FOREVER YOUNG

How to Fight the Aging Process

Dr. Sukhraj S. Dhillon, Ph. D.

New Edge
Publishing
Mountain House, CA, USA

Other Titles and their ISBNs under Self-help and Spiritual Series:
"The Power of Breathing" (ISBN: 978-1466371545)
"A Simple Solution to America's Weight Problem" (ISBN: 978-1466377127)
"Art of Stress-Free Living:" (ISBN: 1413795064)
"Forever Young" (ISBN: 978-1466392069)
"A New Look at Vegetarianism:" (ISBN: 1575150298)
"Health, Happiness & Longevity:" (ISBN: 0870405276)
"Soul and Reincarnation" (ISBN: 978-1466395930)
"Science, Religion & Spirituality" (ISBN: 1424111269)
"In Search of God" (ISBN: 978-1466398498)
"A Treasure of Great Spiritual Stories" (ISBN: 978-1466394773)
"Industrial Leaks and Air Pollution:" (ISBN: 9997691547)
"Cigarette Smoking:" (ISBN: 9997691547)

First Printing: October 2011

ISBN-13: 978-1466392069
ISBN-10: 1466392061

New Edge
Publishing
www.newedgepublishing.com

Printed in U.S.A.

CONTENTS

Introduction

Forever young doesn't mean adding years to your life or for seniors only. It's about helping you function at peak capacity throughout life, feeling great, and being able to do all the things that make life worth living. It's about being biologically or functionally young, regardless of your chronological age.

There is no doubt that prolonging life and staying young is one thing which can have the support of almost every adult in the world. People go through pain and expense to tighten sagging skin, cover a balding scalp, and color gray hair. But prolonged life without the benefits of youth and health is not an adequate achievement. Demand for long life and youthful health actually go back even before the Greek and Roman Empires ruled the world. "When the Greek Goddess of dawn, Eos, begged Zeus to bestow immortality upon her lover, Tithonus, she neglected to ask that he be granted eternal youth as well. So Tithonus grew older and older, yet could not die. Finally out of pity, Eos changed him into a grasshopper."

Today in the twenty-first century we are still exploring approaches to extending the vigorous and productive years of life, and perhaps the best move at this time is to combine ancient eastern approaches with modern western approaches to improve body functions that decline with age. In other words, the dependable solution that has been supported by scientific evidence as well as ancient wisdom is the protection of health from deterioration. The common causes of damage to cells due to stress, poor nutrition, improper breathing and exercise practices are well established and known to most of us. Fortunately, these damages can be considerably reduced by following good nutritional habits along with physical and mental activities. However, the overall health approaches may be supplemented by safe practices based on our knowledge about biological markers of aging, and aging theories.

Vitality and longevity may mean different things to different people. One may have average health and be seeking to increase body potential for mental and physical energy. On the other hand one may be suffering from heart disease or cancer or arthritis or senility, and seeking a cure to these problems. Even among considerably healthy individuals one may be looking for memory and learning capabilities as good as when one was in the early twenties, while others may be looking for passion and slimness as good as when one was a teenager. So every individual has different problems and interests and this guide is intended to harvest the information for everyone who is looking to stay young.

In practicing the suggestions put forward in the pages of this guide, the reader, it is hoped, will be able to enjoy a long disease-free life, full of youth and vitality. When hints in this guide result in a younger appearance, this appearance will not be skin-deep as achieved by cosmetics, but will stem from deep-down improvements in health.

CAUTION: Consult your physician before taking high doses of any chemicals including vitamins and minerals, suggested in this book or otherwise.

Chapter 1

BIOLOGICAL MARKERS OF AGING

According to the National Institute on Aging, biological markers of aging are those physical and behavioral changes that occur at predictable times during the aging process. The identification of these biological markers is important in order to find out about methods or treatment designed to change the rate of aging.

Although there is no universally accepted yardstick for biological or functional age, experts have identified several biomarkers of aging that can be measured by a physician. These include muscular strength, exercise tolerance, vision and hearing, blood pressure, vital capacity (lung function), heart size, and laboratory tests of DHEA, glucose, lipids, and creatinine clearance (kidney function).

In humans, some predictable aging markers that most of us notice are decline in lung capacity and chest expansion, decrease in pupil size, bone loss, sleep variations, alterations in glucose tolerance and immune function, cardiovascular changes, and loss of specific hearing and vision.

Decreased Lung Function

Decreased lung capacity and chest expansion is one of the best indicators of declining health and or aging. These parameters which reflect forced vital capacity (FVC) determine the volume of air one can expel after taking a deep breath. The vital capacity, which is independent of sex, weight, and smoking habits, appears to decline steadily with age in both sexes, falling about 3.8 deciliters per decade in men and 3.1 deciliters per decade in women. The reasons are not clear, but it seems to be related more to chest wall function than to intrinsic factors in the lung function. Other indicators related to decline in breathing capacity show that older adults breathe with greater difficulty and less satisfaction than in earlier years. Past 40 years of age the basal metabolic rate (oxygen consumption) slowly declines until about 80 years of age when a very rapid decline is noted. As a result of decline in metabolic rate, older people get tired easier (as we normally notice). Further discussion on this topic and methods of maintaining breathing efficiency is given in chapter 5 on "Breathing and Longevity."

Pupil Size

Studies of the age-related contraction of the pupil have indicated that as we age, changes in pupil and lens reduce the light available to our retina. The retina of a 20-year-old person may be receiving three times as much light as the retina of a 40-year-old. Moreover, the speed of adjustment to light change also declines with increasing age---in addition to reduced illumination due to smaller pupil sizes. Robert Sekuler and his colleagues from Northwestern University in Illinois found in a study on 120 volunteers ranging in age from 21 to 81 that on average, the subjects age 55 or over had 3 mm pupils and younger than 55 had 4 mm pupils. It is not known why pupil size decreases with advancing age. The possible causes may include atrophy of the dilator muscle fibers, deposition of a hyaline substance below the iris sphincter muscles, or loss of photoreceptors feeding the pupillary light reflex.

Farsightedness (need for reading glasses) is another vision-related functional change generally associated with age. Many people need glasses when they approach age 40 to 45. The reason for a decreasing ability to focus on near objects with advancing age probably results from changes in the lens and the muscular forces acting upon it.

Bone Loss

Decrease in bone mass is probably responsible for the bulk of fractures in older people. Peak bone mass (maximum cortical thickness and cross sectional area) is reached sometime between age 30 and 40, thereafter, loss occurs slowly, averaging 0.3% per year. It is the bone mass which determines the risk for fracture in old age. The peak bone mass, however, is determined by genetic, mechanical, and nutritional factors and it varies in different individuals. Therefore, the risk of fracture due to bone loss is variable in different people depending upon their bone mass.

The cause of age-related bone loss is not certain and is perhaps due to decline in physical activity, decline in muscle mass, and decline in imposed mechanical loads on the skeleton. Bone loss caused by long-term bed-rest and weightlessness, which may be repairable by assuming physical activity, indicates that keeping up physical activity is a helpful hint to slow down this age-related problem. Increase in calcium intake (e.g. by drinking milk or taking calcium supplements) is extremely helpful in delaying bone loss.

Sleep Variations

Sleep parameters that show a substantial change with age include time spent in bed, total sleep time and number of arousals after sleep onset. Studies show that older people spend more time at night lying in bed without being able to sleep. They also spend more time during the day in bed resting or napping than younger subjects do. The studies on total sleep time among older people are conflicting. However, the number of awakenings is clearly higher in older than young people. The frequency of sleeplessness increases with age as given in Table 1.1. Researchers have found that many awakenings are due to breathing disturbances among healthy, elderly individuals. The importance of breathing (chapter 5) again comes into the picture here as a component of youthful health. Very little research has been conducted on biological rhythms in human adults as a function of age, an area of possible great interest.

Table 1.1. Increase in sleeplessness by age.

Age (years)	Frequency of Sleeplessness
18-19	8%
30-34	10%
45-59	21%
60 and over	26%

Some Physiological Changes Related to Aging

The changes listed below are common indicators that we are growing old. These in fact are all too familiar to most of us.

Skin and Hair: A gradual loss of elastic tissue (and of fat and muscle tissue beneath the skin) causes the skin to sag and wrinkle as we age. Weakened blood capillaries often cause the skin to bruise more easily, and harmless burst blood vessels may produce red patches on the hands. Gray hair is the most common change associated with growing old. Thinning of hair is also noticed.

Skeleton and Muscles: Loss of stature and reduction in height occurs. Old people lose height because of the 'shrinking' of the discs between the vertebrae. Loss of elasticity in the connective tissue causes the joints to stiffen and enlarge. The bones become more brittle. Muscles lose some of their bulk and tone in older people. The result is the diminished size of muscles and loose skin. The easy test for muscle change is grip strength which declines with age. In simple words, Muscles atrophy and bones weaken with age.

Heart and Circulation: The heart weakens with age and the network of arteries that circulate blood can accumulate deposits that choke off the flow of blood. The arteries harden and thicken inside. This means that blood circulates less freely. There is some reduction in the supply of oxygen to the tissues, and a poor response to any sudden demand for an increased burst of energy.

The heart, which becomes less efficient with age, has to work even harder to pump blood through the narrowed arterial pathways, and this may cause the blood pressure to rise. These circulatory changes, combined with changes in the skin, mean that old people feel more cold.

Abdominal Organs: The capacity of the abdominal organs is less, and they are less ready to process vast quantities of food. The kidneys, too, become slower to filter impurities from the blood.

Brain and Nervous System: The brain shrinks with age; the significance of this is unknown, since intellectual powers are usually not affected, but short-term memory fails. The main threat to the brain is shortage of oxygen, due to the impaired blood supply. The reaction time of the nerves increases, making responses slower.

Many changes occur in brain cells and function over time. Neurological diseases such as Alzheimer's and Parkinson's manifest themselves in the older body.

Senses: Some sensory loss is to be expected, but not a total shut-down. The two most common effects are a reduced ability to focus on near-by objects and a degree of hearing loss (particularly for the higher tones). Impairment of hearing with advancing age ranks second only to arthritis. The most common source of hearing deficiency is suggested to be a progressive bilateral loss of hearing (presbycusis) for tones and speech due to degenerative physiological changes in the auditory system. Taste, smell and touch are diminished to some degree, and the mechanisms of balance become less accurate.

Other: Other self-explanatory and obvious changes include loss of teeth, increased weight, decline in sex drive.

Other Markers of Aging

Glucose regulation: With age, some people develop diabetes, a chronic disease involving an insulin deficiency and a loss of the body's ability to regulate sugar in blood and urine.

Endocrine function - The body's system of glands, which secrete helpful chemicals into the blood, becomes less efficient with time.

The immune system - The natural system of defenses mounted by the body to combat foreign organisms like viruses, bacteria and parasites begins to let down its guard as we grow old.

Oxidative stress - Life-giving oxygen, paradoxically, can be bad for health. Oxygen sometimes manifests itself as free radicals, toxic ionized oxygen molecules that roam cells disrupting other molecules in a cascade of cellular events that may be at the very root of the aging process.

In addition to changes in immune function, glucose intolerance, cardiovascular function, other changes due to aging include amino acid racemization, the autonomic nervous system, and psychomotor indices, discussed at the National Institute on Aging conference, Bethesda, Maryland in 1981.

Some do-it-yourself tests of Biological or Functional age

Forever young isn't about living forever. It's about helping you function at peak capacity throughout life, feeling great, and being able to do all the things that make life worth living. It's about being biologically young, regardless of your chronological age. You know your chronological age, even if you'd rather not admit to it. But do you know your biological or functional age?

We have given below some tests of functional age. Do it for fun with your family and see how people of different ages score.

Reaction Time

If you've ever been bested by your children or grandchildren in a videogame, you know that reaction time slows down as we age. To test yours, take the **falling-ruler test**. Have someone dangle a ruler from the end, holding it at the 12" or 18" mark (depending on the size of the ruler). Position your thumb and middle finger about 3" inches apart at equal distance on either side of the bottom of the ruler (the 0" mark).

As the other person drops the ruler, without warning, catch it between your thumb and finger as quickly as possible, and note where you caught it. Repeat three times and average your scores. Averages generally go from the 6" mark at age 20-30, to 10" at age 40-50, and 12" or more at age 60.

Visual Accommodation

As we age, the lenses of our eyes stiffen and lose their ability to accommodate, or change shape, and this interferes with near vision.

To test your visual accommodation, hold this page at arm's length and slowly move it towards your eyes until the print suddenly begins to blur. (If you wear glasses for distance, you may use them, but do not use reading glasses.) For the average 21-year-old, the blurring point will be about 4 inches from the eyes; at age 30, 5" inches; at 40, 9 inches; and at 50, 15 inches. By the time you're 60, your arms probably aren't long enough to bring it into focus at all! (The distance for blurring may not be exact depending upon print size. But this gives you an idea.)

Skin Elasticity

One of the most visible markers of aging is the skin. Loss of connective tissue in the skin contributes to the sagging and wrinkling that are characteristic of aging. A reliable test of skin elasticity is to pinch the skin on the back of your hand between your thumb and forefinger for 5 seconds, then see how long it takes to return to normal.

This will take less than a second for most people under 30, and 2-5 seconds for those ages 40-50. However, by age 60, traces of the skin fold will remain for an average of 10-15 seconds, and by age 70, 35-55 seconds.

Static Balance

Static balance is the process by which we maintain an upright posture while standing. Age-related changes in the complex interplay between sensory, nervous, and motor systems are one reason why older people are more prone to falling. When your eyes are closed, the differences in static balance between young and old are exaggerated (older people are more dependent on vision for balance), so this test is one of the most dramatic of all biomarkers.

Stand on a hard, uncarpeted floor, barefoot or in low-heeled shoes. Close your eyes and, bending at the knee, lift one foot (the right foot if you are right-handed, the left if you are left-handed) about 6 inches off the ground. Do not move or hop about to maintain your balance - just stand there with your eyes closed. (Have someone nearby to time you and help you if you start to fall.) See how long you can stand on one leg before putting your foot back down. Repeat two more times and average your scores. The mean score at age 20 is 30 seconds; at age 30, 25 seconds; age 40, 15 seconds; age 50, 10 seconds; age 60, 7 seconds; and age 70, 5 seconds.

Lung Function

Lung function also declines with age. There are several tests of lung function, but one you can do yourself is the match test. Light a match and hold it about 12 inches from your mouth. Inhale deeply, and with your mouth open wide (do not pucker up as you normally would to blow out a candle) attempt to blow out the match. Bring the match forward gradually and repeat until you are able to extinguish the flame. Most 20- to 30-year-olds can do this at a distance of more than 10" from the mouth. For ages 40-50, the average is 7-8", and for 60-70 years, it is 5" or less.

Recommendations: Have fun with these tests, and remember that the results are only broad indicators of where you are right now. Record your results today, make a concentrated effort to improve your overall health, follow the suggestions in this book, and then take these tests again in six and 12 months. Don't be surprised if, despite the passage of time, your functional age gets younger.

Chapter 2

AGING THEORIES

Our bodies are made up of cells that number in the billions. The energy we use to perform any action is generated by metabolic reactions of individual cells. The cells are born, they multiply, they age, they die. One of the most prominent notions in experimental *gerontology* (science of aging) has been that organisms including ourselves age because cells age. For example, why women live longer than men may lie in this notion?

Why Women Live Longer: If there are any men left who still believe that women are the weaker sex, it is long past time for them to think again. With respect to that most essential proof of robustness—the power to stay alive—women are tougher than men from birth through to extreme old age. The average man may run a 100-meter race faster than the average woman and lift heavier weights. But nowadays women outlive men by about five to six years. By age 85 there are roughly six women to every four men. At age 100 the ratio is more than two to one. And by age 122—the current world record for human longevity—the score stands at one-nil in favor of women.

So why do women live longer than men? One idea is that men drive themselves to an early grave with all the hardship and stress of their working lives. If this were so, however, then in these days of greater gender equality, you might expect the mortality gap would vanish or at least diminish. Yet there is little evidence that this is happening. Women today still outlive men by about as much as their stay-at-home mothers outlived their office-going fathers a generation ago. Furthermore, who truly believes that men's work-lives back then were so much more damaging to their health than women's home lives? Just think about the stresses and strains that have always existed in the traditional roles of women: a woman's life in a typical household can be just as hard as a man's. Indeed, statistically speaking, men get a much better deal out of marriage than their wives—married men tend to live many years longer than single men, whereas married women live only a little bit longer than single women. So who actually has the easier life?

It might be that women live longer because they develop healthier habits than men—for example, smoking and drinking less and choosing a better diet. But the number of women who smoke is growing and plenty of others drink and eat unhealthy foods. In any case, if women are so healthy, why is it that despite their longer lives, women spend more years of old age in poor health than men do? The lifestyle argument therefore does not answer the question either.

Let us approach this issue from a wider biological perspective, by looking at other animals. It turns out that the females of most species live longer than the males. This phenomenon suggests that the explanation for the difference within humans might lie deep in our biology.

Many scientists believe that the aging process is caused by the gradual buildup of a huge number of individually tiny faults—some damage to a DNA strand here, a deranged protein molecule there, and so on. This degenerative buildup means that the length of our lives is regulated by the balance between how fast new damage strikes our cells and how efficiently this damage is corrected. The body's mechanisms to maintain and repair our cells are wonderfully effective—which is why we live as long as we do—but these mechanisms are not perfect. Some of the damage passes unrepaired and accumulates as the days, months and years pass by. We age because our bodies keep making mistakes.

We might well ask why our bodies do not repair themselves better. Actually we probably could fix damage better than we do already. In theory at least, we might even do it well enough to live forever. The reason we do not, is because it would have cost more energy than it was worth when our aging process evolved long ago, when our hunter-gatherer ancestors faced a constant struggle against hunger. Under the pressure of natural selection to make the best use of scarce energy supplies, our species gave higher priority to growing and reproducing than to living forever. Our genes treated the body as a short-term vehicle, to be maintained well enough to grow and reproduce, but not worth a greater investment in durability when the chance of dying an accidental death was so great. In other words, genes are immortal, but the body—what the Greeks called SOMA—is disposable.

What causes cells to become senescent or aged, however, is still an open question, confronting various theories. Some of the prominent theories are discussed below in this chapter.

Genetic Theory of Aging

Let us consider first the popular *genetic theory of aging.* Among other things, cells contain nucleic acids, namely DNA (deoxyribonucleic acid) and RNA (ribonucleic acid). Working together these nucleic acids are fundamental to the life process. DNA in the nucleus tells RNA on the periphery how to build particular enzyme-proteins to carry out necessary functioning of the cell, which provides energy and vitality to the organism. As we age, the quality of these nucleic acids deteriorates. There is a DNA repair system built into each cell. If, however, the damage to DNA is too subtle for the repair system to detect or if it accumulates faster than the repair system functions, the cell will gradually become defective in essential control systems or enzymes. This situation will be particularly serious for cells that do not divide after they have differentiated to their mature forms. These include brain and muscle cells. If such cells function poorly or die, they are not replaced. Nucleic acid damage may be less serious for dividing cells such as those of the liver or the lining of the gastrointestinal tract because the process of dividing provides a constant source of new cells. Age-related damage of DNA in both animals and plants is reported in many recent studies. According to genetic theory, therefore, aging is due primarily to the damage of DNA, and thus slowing down aging means keeping the DNA healthy, as discussed later, in this guide.

Free Radicals Theory of Aging

Aging, according to the second prominent *free radicals theory,* is caused by free radicals and oxidative processes (Table 2.1). You might have heard about this theory in relation to vitamin E, which is associated with energy and potency. Actually vitamin E is an antioxidant which interferes with reactions mediated by free radicals and oxidation reactions. Free radicals are missing an electron. For this reason, they are highly reactive entities, which can damage cell membranes, DNA, and other cell structures.

Table 2.1. Life span compared with rate of brain tissue oxidation and free radical formation.

	Lifespan Potential (Years)	Rate of Oxidation
Primates		
Human	90	2.08
Orangutan	50	6.85
Chimpanzee	48	6.62
Baboon	35	7.57
African Green Monkey	34	6.91
Marmoset	20	6.94
Squirrel Monkey	18	8.32
Non-Primates		
Cow	30	6.49
Dog	20	8.24
Rabbit	12	9.60
Deer Mouse	6	19.10
Rat	4	15.50

Field Mouse	3.5	23.10

*The rate of oxidation determines free radical formation and is one measure of the process that scientists think contributes to aging. Lower rates of oxidation suggest fewer oxygen radicals, known to damage cells and contribute to dysfunctions associated with aging.

SOURCE: Modified from Richard G. Cutler, Proceedings of the National Academy of Sciences, July, 1985.

Lots of free radicals are created in cells as they produce energy. Free radicals disrupt a cell's DNA and protein synthesis and repair mechanisms. The Berkeley biologist Bruce Ames has calculated that oxygen radicals damage the DNA inside each cell some 10,000 times per day.

Each time a cell replicates, it copies all of the billions of DNA base pairs that comprise its genome. Cells are very crowded and chemically energetic places, so miscopying sometimes occurs. Fortunately, evolution has devised molecular machines that can rapidly read and then correct most of the copying mistakes, keeping the cells to a fantastically accurate rate of one error per billion nucleotide replications. However, each time the repair mechanisms miss a mistake, it becomes encoded in the DNA -- and the next time duplication occurs, the miscopied DNA is treated as correct. As a result, errors accumulate over time. Miscopied genes lead to the production of distorted proteins, which are inefficient when they work at all. The accumulated molecular damage causes a 0.5 percent decline per year in overall physical capacity after age 30.

Increasingly, researchers are focusing their attention on the damage free radicals cause in the tiny energy-producing organelles called **mitochondria** (where oxygen is utilized during respiration/ breathing). Like any other power plant, mitochondria produce not just energy but also wastes and pollution, including copious free radicals. As good as mitochondria are at mopping these up, some of them nevertheless get loose and damage the tiny DNA genomes at the heart of the mitochondria. Free radicals create a cellular death spiral by mutating mitochondrial DNA, which in turn degrades their energy production and increases the production of free radicals, refueling the cycle.

Other research points to another process **linking** free radicals to aging. Apparently, we are literally cooking ourselves to death. In cooking, sugars and proteins stick together to form tasty brown crusts like those on French toast. Our own metabolisms are a form of low-temperature cooking that causes sticky sugars such as glucose to cross-link with proteins to create advanced *glycation* end products (called AGEs or ADVANCED GLYCATION END PRODUCTS). AGEs may be formed external to the body (exogenously) by heating (e.g., cooking); or inside the body (endogenously) through normal metabolism and aging. AGEs are biological junk that accumulates in cells, interfering with their functions over time. For example, AGEs reduce the elasticity and flexibility of the collagen in our ligaments. They are also linked to diabetes and to cardiovascular disease.

In a related process, our cells' recycling centers, called lysosomes, become clogged with cross-linked proteins and other cellular rubbish. This cellular gunk is called lipofuscin. Lipofuscin-filled lysosomes slowly crowd and hinder other cellular functions.

Another process involving free radicals is inflammation. Inflammation occurs when our immune system cells drench invaders such as bacteria and viruses with free radicals to rip them apart. The problem is that sometimes the inflammatory attacks don't ratchet down when the threat is gone, and our immune cells keep pumping out free radicals. Chronic inflammation has been linked to many diseases associated with aging, including arthritis, atherosclerosis, diabetes, Alzheimer's, and cancer.

As mentioned above, free radicals may either be produced by cells as a result of their metabolic processes or they may come from the environment. For example, eating foods which have been exposed to X-rays, cosmic rays and nuclear fallout could carry free radicals into our body. The use of X-rays to sterilize foods for storing (you may have seen in news media including TV shows like 20/20 and Good Morning America) should be considered with caution. The claim that using X-rays is similar to exposing foods to heat is true. However, the possibility of free radicals having been formed during the exposure period cannot be ruled out. Free radicals can also be formed by direct exposure of body tissue to radiation. Damage by free radicals to DNA or other cell structures may be caused directly by reacting promiscuously with other molecules, causing them to become free radicals too, or indirectly by generating strong oxidizing agents. The oxidation of a molecule causes it to become less efficient or actually harmful. This, according to the free radical-oxidation theory, is the root cause of aging.

As pointed out earlier, vitamin E, because it is an antioxidant, slows down oxidation and hence is thought to retard aging. Support for the involvement of free radicals and vitamin E therapy in aging has come from the studies of L. Packer, University of California, Berkeley, and J.E. Smith, Veterans Administration Hospital, Martinez, California. They added vitamin E to cultured fibroblasts from human embryos which normally divide about 50 times. But in the presence of vitamin E, the cells continued to divide and to have youthful characteristics for about 120 population doublings; after that they too became senescent and died. The concentration of vitamin E in the enriched culture medium was approximately the same as that in serum *in vivo*.

Note: The natural defense against free radicals is enzymes such as *superoxide dismutase.* But the accumulative damage that cannot be protected by natural enzymes can be reduced by using antioxidants as discussed above.

Calorie Restriction

The free radical theory of aging is backed by more than seven decades of research on calorie restriction which is "under-nutrition without malnutrition." Caloric restriction has been shown to extend both the maximal and average life spans of worms, insects and mice. In 1935 Clive McCay, a professor of nutrition at Cornell, noted that if laboratory rats are fed only about two-thirds of the food they would freely choose to eat, their life spans increase by 40 percent to 50 percent. This result has been confirmed many times since then. Researchers think that semi-starvation may make metabolic processes more efficient, producing fewer free radicals and also perhaps boosting cells' DNA repair systems, since the hungry organism may have to live longer in order to reproduce.

The theory behind caloric restriction is based on metabolism rates. Imagine every individual is given a set amount of life to live. The more you eat, the higher your metabolism and the faster you burn through your life, shortening your lifespan. Conversely, the less you eat, the lower your metabolism and the slower you burn through your life, as a consequence extending your time here on earth.

Researchers at the University of Washington in 2005 found that the link between caloric restriction and longevity is related to a genetic pathway in yeast cells. The University of Washington researchers first identified the genes that regulate lifespan in yeast, then tested two of these genes for their connection to caloric restriction. They found that by mutating a gene linked to nutrient uptake, they could increase the yeast cell's lifespan. The mutation is similar to reducing the calories that the yeast cell gets.

The regulation of insulin might explain the benefits of restricting calories. The gene makes a signaling protein that regulates insulin and insulin-like growth factor (IGF-1) pathways, and has also been found to affect lifespan in other model organisms.

"Having this pathway implicated in lifespan is consistent with the theory about insulin/IGF-1 response in animals and humans," explains Matt Kaeberlein, one of the UW researchers conducting the study. "That theory basically says that high nutrient levels make the organism grow faster and bigger, but also reduce lifespan. This may be one reason why calorie-restricted mice live longer, but are smaller than other mice."

Cellular respiration, the process of turning food into energy, produces free radicals that are very reactive within the cell. These can damage DNA, organelles, and other important cellular components. The higher an individual's rate of metabolism, the more free radicals the organism produces. Caloric restriction seems to put the brakes on some of these degenerative processes that take place in cells and tissues with aging.

Though studies on mice and yeast have shown that caloric restriction can increase life span, human societies often mirror the results. Okinawa, Japan, is a longevity hot spot with one of the highest concentrations of centenarians. One of their traditional sayings is *"hara hachi bu,"* or eat until you are 80% full.

Probably the most promising immediate thing you can do to increase your chances of seeing your great-grandchildren is to stop eating so much. **Calorie restriction** is the only known technique for increasing the life spans of many different organisms. The foremost advocate of this approach is probably the UCLA biologist Roy Walford. However, his unrealistic calorie restricted menus are seen by some as dieting to death. Such diets may not really make your life longer, but it will certainly make it feel that way. Never the less, Calorie restriction is a good approach but need to be done sensibly. Add some of the **Vegetarian recipes** to your diet.

Barbara Hansen, a diabetes researcher at the University of Maryland, has spent 20 years investigating the effects of calorie restriction on rhesus monkeys. The experiment has not run long enough to determine if the ultimate life spans of the calorie-restricted monkeys will be increased. But on several related issues, her findings are unequivocal: When she compares old calorie-restricted monkeys to old monkeys that eat what they want, the calorie-restricted ones do not have heart disease, diabetes, or hypertension, and their cholesterol is lower. They're healthier.

There is no question that maintaining a reasonable weight prevents the onset of many illnesses associated with aging. But what if you find the notion of living without burger and pepperoni pizza unbearable? Is there hope for you?

There may be. Hansen hopes that by starving monkeys she can pave the way to a pill providing all the health benefits of calorie restriction while allowing you to consume all the ice cream and beer you want. She has identified a compound that affects the PPAR-Delta receptor, which improves the body's response to insulin and glucose, mimicking the benefits of calorie restriction. It is now in early testing by Glaxo.

Calorie restriction research could also help us discover aging's elusive biomarkers. With the sequencing of the human genome and the advent of chip gene technologies, researchers can monitor the simultaneous actions of thousands of genes in tissues. The aim is to characterize the differences between the gene activity in tissues from old people and the gene activity in tissues from young people. Already, chip tests have found that the gene expression of tissues taken from old, calorie-restricted mice is similar to that found in young mice.

Among other benefits, finding such biomarkers would be a major advance in testing interventions for their effectiveness in slowing aging. Right now, the only way to see whether a proposed longevity treatment works is to wait for people to die.

Cross-linkage Theory of Aging

Another interesting theory of aging is the *cross-linkage theory of aging,* which emphasizes the effects of doubled or tripled molecules of protein. According to this theory, protein molecules, which are long chains of amino acids, become linked with other protein molecules. These doubled or tripled molecules of protein are unnatural to the body and they gum up the cells with useless endangering debris. In addition to cross-linkage between protein molecules, cross-linkage between DNA molecules also forms a part of the theory. When cross linkages form between the strands of DNA, they can interfere with the functioning of DNA in ways discussed as part of the genetic theory of aging.

Autoimmune Theory of Aging

Another popular theory of aging, *autoimmune aging,* suggests that with age some alterations occur in the body's immunological defense reaction, and the host attacks its own kind. As you know, the body's immune system protects it from disease and cancer. The major components of the immune system are two types of white blood cells, B cells and T cells. The main job of the B cells is to fight bacteria and virus attacks by releasing proteins called antibodies. The main job of the T cells is to attack and destroy cells foreign to the body, such as cancer cells and transplant cells. Dr. Roy Walford of UCLA suggests that T cells malfunction with age, and as a result cancer increases as people get older because the T cells no longer vigorously attack cancer cells. Another result is that B and T cells behave abnormally, attacking not only disease organisms and cancer cells, but body's own normal, healthy cells. This destruction of the body by its own protective immune system, as stated above, is called auto-immunity.

The spleen which is a reservoir for red blood cells, protects the body during an accident. It is also a reservoir for the T cells which protect against invasion by foreign cells. Dr. T. Makinodian of the National Institute on Aging, showed that removal of the spleen increased life span in mice. He suggests that this result is due to the fact that T cells in older individuals can become defective and cause autoimmune aging. However, the spleen is still required because some of the functional T cells would be needed to fight disease and cancer cells. Makinodian further modified his experiment to determine that transfusion of T cells from the young animals could prolong age and fight disease.

It has also been suggested that autoimmune aging can be slowed or reversed by the use of thymosin, a hormone produced by the thymus which may be responsible for maintaining the function of T cells.

Removal of the spleen or use of the hormone thymosin are still too much in the experimental stage to be applied in prolonging human life. However, following a diet to slow autoimmune aging is practical (as discussed later in this book).

Love and Death

Reproduction and death, it turns out, are inextricably intertwined. "It doesn't pay to have a body that will last forever," notes Austad. "Evolution only cares about reproduction." Every body harbors a line of immortal cells: the germ cells that produce eggs and sperm. Germ cells migrate from body to body down the millennia, disposing of their worn-out carriers as they move on. Once your ovaries or testes are done with you, they couldn't care less whether you live.

Here, then, is the definitive answer to the eternal question: Which came first, the chicken or the egg? The egg did. A chicken is merely an egg's way of making more eggs.

In the case of human beings, evolution has selected for a set of genes that keep our bodies in pretty good shape long enough to mature sexually, produce progeny, and raise those progeny to sexual maturity. Time elapsed is about 40 years. The evolutionary insight here is that if a body invests a lot of energy in repairing itself, it will reduce the amount it can devote to reproduction. That may be good for individual bodies, but your germ cells have no interest in keeping you forever young.

The UCLA biologist Michael Rose firmly established the evolutionary connection between sex and death by breeding fruit flies. Rose selected only those flies that reproduced late in life and bred them with one another. The longer it took the insects to reproduce, the longer they lived. Rose now has flies that live 130 days instead of the usual 40.

The connection was further bolstered by Cynthia Kenyon, a biologist at the University of California at San Francisco. Kenyon reported that she could double the life spans of nematode worms by removing their germ-line stem cells -- the cells that produce eggs and sperm. Then there's Lawrence Donehower's research at Baylor Medical College. Donehower has found that the genes that are helpful in guaranteeing a robust youth are harmful in the long run. The tumor-suppressing p53 gene keeps us from developing cancers in early life, but at the cost of stimulating our immune systems to destroy over time the reserve of rapidly dividing stem cells that replenish our tissues. As our stem cells are killed off, our tissues deteriorate. The result of this "antagonistic pleiotropy" is aging.

Another example of antagonistic pleiotropy was discovered by the biologist Leonard Hayflick in 1961. Hayflick, later at U.C. San Francisco, found that human cells in vitro would divide only 50 to 80 times, then stop. For a while, some researchers thought this "Hayflick limit" might be the key to aging. What it appears to be is an evolved mechanism to prevent cancer? Cancer is the uncontrolled proliferation of cells, and as cells divide they often accumulate errors that predispose them toward becoming cancerous. If there is a limit on the number of times a cell can divide, such a limit prevents cells from eventually mutating into cancer cells.

How do cells know when to stop? Through **telomeres**, caps composed of repetitive DNA sequences at the ends of chromosomes. These function somewhat like the aglets on the ends of shoelaces that keep them from unraveling. Through a peculiarity in DNA replication, each time a cell divides, its daughter cells lose a tiny bit of their telomeres. Once the telomeres are gone, the cell stops dividing and becomes senescent.

Two types of cells that do not suffer this problem. One is the germ cells that are the progenitors of sperm and eggs. Their telomeres are restored by an enzyme specific for restoring telomeres, making them essentially immortal. The other group is cancer cells. They can divide without limit, which is what makes them so deadly.

Significant aging is a relatively new phenomenon. Over evolutionary history, once creatures began to falter in any way, they were eaten or dropped dead of disease -- eaten by bacteria, as it were -- so they never had a chance to get old. "As soon as an animal in the wild starts to slow down even a little bit, it's eliminated from the population very quickly," says Simon Melov, a researcher at the Buck Institute, a nonprofit organization devoted to aging research. "Aging is not a natural state for us either," he adds. "The evidence we have indicates that 10,000 to 20,000 years ago, most people didn't live much past 30." Today, the only creatures that actually experience aging are human beings and the animals they protect, such as pets and livestock.

Telomeres and Aging

Since this is a comparatively new but promising theory, the details are presented for those who will be interested in science behind this theory. It is also close to my own research in molecular biology. If not interested, you may skip details. Telomeres now are well known units of molecular cell system. They play great role in cell life cycle regulation, sometimes they are called molecular clock of the cell. Lets review the history of telomeres, how everything started?

The cells: In 1908, A. Carrel, a Nobel prize-winning surgeon, became interested in the growth of cells in culture, in 1912; he established a culture of chick heart fibroblast cells, which he then grew in the laboratory for 34 years. This work led to the general acceptance of the notion that vertebrate cells can divide indefinitely in culture. As individual cells were immortal, Carrel reasoned that aging is "an attribute of the multicellular body as a whole". In 1961, this concept of cell immortality was challenged by experiments published by Hayflick and Moorehead. They found that fibroblast cultures derived from human skin would divide 40 to 50 times, and then stop and "undergo senescence". Further work showed that cells from older people underwent fewer divisions than cells from younger people, suggesting that it was the total number or divisions since birth, not total divisions in culture that was important. When subsequent work showed that Carrel's immortal chicken cell cultures were not reproducible, Hayflick's senescence model eventually became accepted.

Two important questions emerged from the nascent field of cellular senescence. First, what is the role of cellular senescence in humans? Does the limited capacity of cells to divide relate to human aging, or it is a mechanism to prevent tumor formation? Second, what tells cells to stop dividing?

The telomere: In 1978, Blackburn, working in Gall's laboratory at Yale, was interested in determining the DNA sequence that allowed the *Tetrahymena* rDNA molecule to be maintained as a linear chromosome. Her work led to the finding that chromosome ends, or telomeres, are made of simple repeat DNA sequences. It soon became apparent that this motif was conserved throughout evolution and that a common mechanism might exist in eukaryotes for the maintenance of telomeres. In 1984, working in Blackburn's laboratory, Carol W. Greider identified an enzyme, telomerase that added telomere repeats onto chromosome ends. He suggested that telomerase would compensate for the incomplete replication of chromosome ends. This would explain the telomere length maintenance seen in organisms such as *Tetrachymena* and yeast. Telomerase is an unusual polymerase; it contains an integral RNA component that provides the template for synthesis of telomere repeats.

The connection: Insight into the molecular structure of the ends of human chromosomes came from using a probe representing a sequence on the Y chromosome that was near enough to the telomere to follow the terminal chromosome fragment. Using this probe, Cooke found that telomeres in germ line tissue (sperm) were longer than telomeres in somatic tissue (blood cells). He speculated that telomere length is tissue-specific and that telomere length shortens between germ line and somatic tissues. Subsequently, the identification of the simple-sequence telomere repeat from human, cells allowed a simple analysis of telomere length and cell senescence. Harley, Furcher, and Greider then found that telomeres indeed shorten as normal human fibroblasts grow in culture.

Telomeres were also shorter in skin samples from older people than from younger people, suggesting that the shortening was not a tissue culture phenomenon. At about the same time, Hastie and de Lange found that tumor samples had shorter telomeres than adjacent normal tissue, providing the first suggestion of a connection between telomeres and cancer.

The synthesis: In the early 1990s, a model emerged which had two parts: one that linked telomeres to cell senescence, and the other that linked telomeres, telomerase and cancer. The model stated that telomeres shorten during growth of primary fibroblasts, because of the end replication problem and the absence of telomerase. Germ line cells, in contrast, have telomerase and thus maintain telomere length. Telomere shortening signals cells, to senescence. Senescence however can be bypassed by expression of viral oncogenes. During this extended life span, telomeres continue to shorten until the cell culture reaches a crisis. At crisis many cells die. The few cells that survive, can divide indefinitely. These cells have activated telomerase and maintain or even elongate telomeres. With the demonstration that tumor cells, like immortal cells in culture, express the enzyme, telomerase was proposed as a potential target for anti-cancer therapy. The reports by Bodner, Vaziri and Benchimol provided strong evidence for the first part of this hypothesis that **telomere shortening is a mechanism that limits cell division capacity.**

Later what they found was hTERT gene. The initial surprise was that simply expressing hTERT in primary cells led to telomerase activity. Although telomerase is composed of both protein and RNA, the RNA component is often present even in cells that do not normally have activity. Apparently, this level of RNA was sufficient for telomerase activity when hTERT was present. The next surprise was that the presence of telomerase activity in primary cells was sufficient for telomere elongation. Although it was the result that many had hoped for, as evidence suggested that the availability of telomere-binding proteins might limit telomere growth. At last the experiment was made: the frequency of senescent primary cell clones was compared between cell that had telomerase activity and those that did not. **Cells with longer telomeres did not undergone senescence, whereas those with short telomeres did. So it was**

concluded and showed that telomere length was one criterion that determinate entry into cell senescence.

So **telomeres** and telomerase became the object of **gerontology**, oncology, cell biology etc.

Conclusion: Telomeres cap the ends of chromosomes, the structures that carry genes. Every time a cell divides, the telomeres get shorter. When the telomeres get too short, the cell can no longer divide and dies.

But here's a news flash: **Exercise** actually does make you younger-- right down to your DNA as indicated by size of **telomeres**. When researchers examined the lifestyle habits and DNA of more than 2,400 twins, they found that regular exercisers had significantly longer telomeres (a region of DNA that acts as a biological marker for aging) than their sedentary peers. Those who exercised a little less than 30 minutes a day had telomeres that looked 10 years younger than those who did just 16 minutes a week. (Lynn F. Cherkas etal, Arch Intern Med. 2008;168(2):154-158)

It now appears that physically active people have cells that look younger at the molecular level than those that are sedentary showing changes in Telomere length.

Other Theories

Other theories of aging include breakdown of the brain pacemaker, damage of cell membranes, loss of collagen elasticity, and so on. As you see, none of the theories (based on individual experiments) are conclusive and aging perhaps is a result of several factors that influence body functioning.

The vagueness and experimental stage of these theories limit their immediate practical value. The best we can do is to use some of the practical tips provided by the aging theories. The tips based on theories are given in later chapters. The dependable solution that has been supported by scientific evidence, as well as ancient experiences, is protecting the health from deterioration. The common causes of damage to cells due to stress, poor nutrition, improper breathing and exercise practices, however, are well established and known to most of us. Fortunately, these damages can be considerably reduced, by following good nutritional habits along with physical and mental activity. We know that people who are young have eager, inquisitive minds. They are curious, always seeking and evaluating answers. They are willing to try something new--a new approach to a job, a new kind of music, a new response to a recurring situation. Youngsters laugh and enjoy themselves, they play and have fun. If you had those same qualities, attributes and attitudes, you too would be young at any age.

Chapter 3

LIFE STYLE AND LONGEVITY

It is not merely about the year that adds up to your age but the effects of it to your physical, mental, and emotional wellbeing. There are two ways to age: aging happily and aging sadly. Your choice will reflect how well you will enjoy the process.

Yes, the power to choose between aging gracefully and aging miserably is in your hands. It cannot be stressed enough that you need to make the choice early in life to enjoy the full benefits in the long run.

Secrets of Centenarians- Pay Attention to Their Stories

There is a rapid growing clan of centenarians, whose numbers in the United States have increased to 96,548 in 2009 from 38,300 in 1990, according to the Census Bureau.

Sallie Clark, 108, a former homemaker, was born in Macon, GA. Currently residing in the Bronx, NY, she is the mother of nine children; four are deceased. Living long must be in her genes because her mother lived to be 102. A missionary in the Pentecostal church, Ms. Clark loves to talk about the Lord. She says that's "what keeps me going." Though she currently resides in a rehab center, she remains active there by praising the Lord as a member of its choir. Her favorite song to sing is Love Lifted Me. She believes in watching her diet and eats mostly lamb's stew, string beans and rice. She also loves to eat corn bread.

BB Hollins, 106, a former roofer, was born and still lives in Jackson, MS. He is the father of 13 children; one is deceased. Mr. Hollins says that living long "runs on his side of the family." His mother died at 110, one sister died at 101 and another sister died at 99. An elder in the Church of God in Christ, Hollins calls church "the joy of my life." He also likes to watch TV and loves sports. His favorite sport to watch is baseball. As a member of the oldest fraternal organization in America, the Prince Hall Masons, he continues to work with the fraternal order that has a religious base. In fact, the lodge that he belongs to recently announced a scholarship in his name.

Mamie J. Rearden, 104, of Edgefield, SC, is a former schoolteacher and the mother of 11 children and two adoptive children. Ms. Rearden likes sewing, crocheting, singing in the choir at the Baptist church she attends, and visiting the sick and the shut-in. She credits her longevity to "not being a gossip and treating everyone the way she wants to be treated."

Leonard Bennett, 103, was born in Pulaski, MS, but now lives in Gulfport. Mr. Bennett is the father of five; one is deceased. A former handyman, he dropped out of school in the fourth grade so that he could work to make money for his family. Though he left school early, Mr. Bennett values education so much so that he made sure that all of his children either graduated from college or attended. He loves watching baseball, especially the Atlanta Braves. Also a member of the Masons, he busies himself by working with the fraternal order. When he's not taking a walk to the barbershop to hang out with his buddies, he likes working in his garden. Church is also important in the deacon and honorary trustee's life. His philosophy for living a long life is "God first, early to bed, early to rise and hard work." Also, he credits "God's grace, homegrown food and eating before you get hungry and going to bed before you get sleepy" to contributors of his peaceful life.

Sadie Stinson, 105, is a native of Grenada, MS, but currently resides in Chicago. She also says living long is in her genes; it's a "West Indian" hereditary thing. But more importantly than that, she credits her longevity to Christian living. She's never smoked, but years ago she admits to using "some kind of tonic." Her sister, Bernice Stinson Lewis, who is 87, says that Sadie is really "106 but Sadie lost count of a year." Ms. Stinson, who never married or had children, is an independent woman. She lives alone and still washes for herself on a scrub board and continues to cook some of her favorite foods, which include turnip greens and hot water corn bread. She doesn't eat much canned foods and loves fresh vegetables. She has most of her own teeth, doesn't wear glasses and still catches the bus everywhere she wants to go. A former seamstress, she still loves to sew and knit.

Katie Rivers-Williamson, 105, a former sharecropper and field hand, is the mother of three; two are deceased. She enjoys sharing her wisdom with others, including the sayings "always keep some cheese (money) tucked away for a rainy day" and "never let your right hand know what your left hand is doing." Ms. Rivers-Williamson credits her secret to a long life to her "strong belief in God and the memories of chasing her grandchildren with a switch in the fields." Her favorite scripture is Psalm 23 and she enjoys singing the song Give Me Wings.

Ida M. Williams, 101, was born and still resides in Columbia, SC. She is the mother of three. A longtime member of the National Council of Negro Women, Ms. Williams loves to read, making sure that she reads two books a week. For 12 years she worked with Meals-On-Wheels, where she seldom missed a day of packing meals. She was featured on the poster for the organization's March for Meals-On-Wheels. When she was 98, she put on her walking shoes and marched for the cause! A deaconess emeritus of a Baptist church, Ms. Williams credits "77 years of love and time to the Lord," as her reason for longevity.

Rebecca Brock Iverson, 100, lives in Baltimore, MD. She also is an independent woman who prefers to live alone. She keeps busy by travelling to a senior citizen center to partake in making arts and crafts. Ms. Iverson loves making quilts and attending church. She is the "mother of the church" at Wayland Baptist Church in Baltimore. When the church announced her birthday, Ms. Iverson was so happy that she "did a dance." The church honored her with a gift that she'll never forget--an all-expenses-paid trip to Disney World in Florida! When Ms. Iverson got to Disney World, she didn't mind sharing the spotlight with another centenarian--Mickey Mouse! It was a delight for her to serve as a grand marshal with Mickey during the famous Disneyland parade. She loves praising the Lord and credits her good health to her "faith in God and the support of her loving family and friends."

Colonel Alfred Thomas, 100, is the father of six children and makes his home in Eufaula, AL. A former chauffeur and caretaker of an estate, Mr. Thomas loves to read the Bible. His sight has declined immensely throughout the years, but thanks to his "photographic" memory, he is able to learn Bible scriptures and verses word for word. Like Mr. Hollins and Mr. Bennett, Mr. Thomas is also a Mason. In fact he is a former Grand Master in the fraternal order. He credits his long life to his "devoted and strong belief in God, good eating habits, not using alcohol or drugs and allowing God to be the source of strength to change the things man is capable of doing, and letting go and letting God."

Luticha Scott, 100, lives in Chicago, but was born in Louisiana. She is the mother of one daughter. Like many of the other centenarian women, Scott also lives alone and cooks for herself. She doesn't believe in seasoning her food and doesn't eat pork. She only eats chicken and fish and lots of vegetables. Her health is near perfect with the exception of taking medicine for her high blood pressure. Ms. Scott believes in eating a banana every day because "it makes me feel good." Ms. Scott is very cautious of her feet and has never owned a pair of house slippers. She believes in protecting and taking care of her feet so she only wears oxford shoes around the house because she believes that the feet must be covered.

Marie Rogers, 100, lives in Emporia, KS, and is the mother of three. A former interior decorator, Rogers has always enjoyed doing things for others. She attributes her long life to teaching by example, being honest and teaching others to be honest and loving God. A longtime member of the NAACP, she is Deaconess Emeritus of a Baptist church in Emporia.

Mamie Mary Douglas, 100, is a former cook who lives in Louisville, KY. Ms. Douglas is also an independent woman who prefers to live alone and still loves to cook. She was once married, but she never had any children. Her philosophy for life is "hard work, good food and being kind to everybody." She also loves to eat Great Northern beans and corn bread. She stands by "having a good warm beer every night before you go to bed because it will help you to sleep, relax you, keep you strong and ward off anything."

Phil Damsky, 100, of Brooklyn, lived most of his life in various Brooklyn neighborhoods. He served as a manager of a shoe store for about 30 years.

Hazel Miller, of Charlotte, N.C., drives 25 miles to Concord every Monday for lessons in painting china porcelain. She is also an avid dancer. "I think it's great to live to be 100," says Hazel Miller. "There's no secret about it. You just don't die. The best part of being 100 is that you lived to be 100. If you can enjoy it, it's an extra good thing." Ms. Miller also explains how she took up line dancing because of a lack of male dancing partners.

Esther Tuttle is nearing the end of the 10th decade of a remarkably productive and adventurous life. She wrote a memoir with the prescient title "No Rocking Chair for Me" displaying an acute memory of events, names, dates and places that she retains as she approaches 100.

What is the secret to her longevity? Is it genetics? Perhaps, but it's hard to say. Her parents died at ages 42 and 50, leaving her an orphan at age 11, along with three siblings, one of whom did live to 96.

Genes do play a role in longevity. Dr. Nir Barzilai, a geneticist at the Albert Einstein College of Medicine in New York, reports that centenarians are 20 times as likely as the average person to have a long-lived relative. But a Swedish study of identical twins separated at birth and reared apart concluded that only about 20 to 30 percent of longevity is genetically determined. Lifestyle seems to be the more dominant factor.

As Mrs. Tuttle said in clarion tones that belie her advanced age: "I am blessed and I've worked on it. You've got to work, be cheerful and look for something fun to do. It's a whole attitude.

"If you respect what the doctors tell you to do, you can live a long life, but you have to do it. You can't ignore the advice."

Her memoir revealed three critical attributes that might be dubbed longevity's version of the three R's: resolution, resourcefulness and resilience. Throughout her long life, she's taken hardships in stride, traipsed blithely over obstacles and converted many into building blocks. And she has adhered to a regimen of a careful diet, hard work, regular exercise and a very long list of community service, all while raising three children.

Like many if not most other centenarians, according to the findings of the New England Centenarian Study at Boston University, Mrs.

Tuttle is an extrovert who has many friends, a healthy dose of self-esteem and strong ties to family and community. She continues to enjoy her youthful passions for the theater and opera.

A study of centenarians in Sardinia found that they tend to be physically active, have extensive social networks and maintain strong ties with family and friends. They are also less likely to be depressed than the average 60-year-old.

Do **optimists** live longer than pessimists? Yes, studies indicate. Dr. Hilary A. Tindle of the University of Pittsburgh Medical Center, found that among 97,000 women followed for eight years, those deemed optimistic were significantly less likely to die from heart disease and all causes than were pessimistic women, whom she described as "cynically hostile."

The optimists were also less likely to have high blood pressure, diabetes or high cholesterol, suggesting they take better care of their health. Indeed, the pessimists were more likely to be overweight, smoke cigarettes and avoid exercise, indicating, Dr. Tindle says, that negative thinkers make poorer lifestyle choices than positive thinkers.

Continuing with lifestyle of Esther Tuttle, she could serve as a model for many findings of various studies. Each morning, she does an hour of **yoga** and other floor exercises, then dresses and goes out on the street or to the top of her Manhattan apartment building for a half-hour **walk** before breakfast. Her usual breakfast: orange juice, oatmeal, a banana and black coffee. Then she works at her desk, mostly corresponding with her 11 grandchildren, 21 great grandchildren and one great-great-grandchild, now 3. "So many birthdays — one or two a month," she said.

Lunch may be soup or leftover meat, a "very thin" slice of rye toast, with tea and Jell-O or fruit for dessert. The afternoon includes an hour's nap and another walk, often combined with grocery shopping.

At 6:30 every evening, she enjoys a cocktail before a home-cooked dinner of lamb, pork chops, roast chicken or "a very good stew" she makes herself. Mrs. Tuttle, whose husband, Ben, died about 20-years back, lives with a dear friend, Allene Hatch, 84, an artist and author affectionately known as Squeaky. "Most days I do the cooking, and Squeaky cleans up afterward."

Stay-at-home evenings are spent reading or watching "a good movie" on television, she said.

Mrs. Tuttle recently gave up a lifelong passion for horseback riding, but she still drives, though not on public roads, only on a 300-acre farm in upstate New York that the Tuttles had the wisdom to acquire when land was cheap. Her children built homes on the property and now live there in retirement, providing Mrs. Tuttle with nearby loving company all summer and during the spring and fall weekends she spends at the farm.

As good as her health is (no high blood pressure, high cholesterol or diabetes), it is not perfect. She describes herself as "a bionic woman from the waist up," with an artificial breast to replace the cancerous one removed 20 years ago, a heart pacemaker installed about a decade ago, a hearing aid and contact lenses.

Although she has spurned dairy foods for most of her life (she still follows the advice of a predecessor of Dr. Robert Atkins who told her to avoid dairy and follow a diet low in carbohydrates and rich in meats and fats), she was only recently found to have osteoporosis, for which she now takes a monthly pill along with daily supplements of calcium and vitamins C and D.

Nor has she always enjoyed an affluent lifestyle. Though born into an accomplished, well-to-do family, her parents' early death (the children were taken in by an aunt with limited means) and her decision to pursue an acting career led to a hardscrabble existence that persisted through the early years of her marriage and life on a farm with three small children and no electricity and makeshift indoor plumbing. According to one study, survivors of traumatic life events **learn to cope better** with stress and poverty and are more likely to live to 100.

In lieu of trauma, there are many measures one can take to facilitate a long, wholesome and productive life. Why live to 100 if those last years will be marred by physical and emotional misery? Many of these are given in "**Art of Stress-free Living**."

Predictors of Reaching 100: Once it truly became apparent that living to 100 was a terrific advantage, not just in years of survival but importantly in many more years of quality life, Boston University School of Medicine, set out to understand what factors the centenarians had in common that might explain such an advantage. Not all centenarians are alike. They vary widely in years of education (no years to post-graduate), socioeconomic status (very poor to very rich), religion, ethnicity and patterns of diet (strictly vegetarian to extremely rich in saturated fats). However, the centenarians Boston University has studied do have a number of characteristics in common:

• Few centenarians are obese. In the case of men, they are nearly always lean.

• Substantial smoking history is rare.

• A preliminary study suggests that centenarians are better able to handle stress than the majority of people.

• Some centenarians (~15%) had no significant changes in their thinking abilities disproved the expectation by many that all centenarians would be demented. The Alzheimer's disease was not inevitable. Some centenarians had very healthy appearing brains.

• Many centenarian women have a history of bearing children after the age of 35 years and even 40 years. A woman who naturally has a child after the age of 40 has a 4 times greater chance of living to 100 compared to women who do not. It is probably not the act of bearing a child in one's forties that promotes long life, but rather, doing so may be an indicator that the woman's reproductive system is aging slowly and that the rest of her body is as well. Such slow aging and the avoidance or delay of diseases that adversely impact reproduction would bode well for the woman's subsequent ability to achieve very old age.

• At least 50% of centenarians have first-degree relatives and/or grandparents who also achieve very old age, and many have exceptionally old siblings. Male siblings of centenarians have a 17 times greater chance than other men born around the same time of reaching age 100 years and female siblings have 8½ times greater chance than other females also born around the same time of achieving age 100.

- Many of the children of centenarians (age range of 65 to 82 years) appear to be following in their parents' footsteps with marked delays in cardiovascular disease, diabetes and overall mortality.

- Some families demonstrate incredible clustering for exceptional longevity that cannot be due to chance and must be due to familial factors that members of these families have in common.

- Based upon standardized personality testing, the offspring of centenarians, compared to population norms, score low in neuroticism and high in extraversion.

- Genetic variation plays a very strong role in exceptional longevity.

While studying habits of long-lived people, Writer and explorer John Robbins cites the powerful link between environment and health, culture and vitality and how they are significant to the aging process. In his bestselling book, Robbins reveals how we can improve not just our lifespan but more importantly, our health span. His study is based from four different cultures that produced the healthiest and happiest longest-living people in the world.

Robbins dug deep into the study of the lifestyle and traditions of four societies -- Abkhazia in South Russia, Vilcabamba in South America, Hunza in Central Asia, and Okinawa in Japan. Those communities are known to produce people who live amazingly well beyond the 100 mark.

The secret is really no secret. People in those societies live well and continue to grow even at old age. The saying that "The sign of old age is when you stop growing" is true in their case. Interestingly, aside from a balanced diet and daily exercise, the significance of strong personal bonds has been singled out.

One of the keys to people's long life is the quality of relationships they are able to build. Robbins discovered strong medical evidence that links a person's healthy interactions with others with his lifespan. Beware, because according to Robbins findings, loneliness can make you look and feel old early.

The Longevity of the People of Southern Russia

National Geographic has been fascinated about certain cultures of the most vibrant elder population. The company commissioned the travel and exploration of Dr. Alexander Leaf from Harvard University so he can share with the world the word about how the elders in those cultures enjoy the youthful glow even at 100.

As a man of Science, Dr. Leaf does not believe in the fountain of youth. He knows there is nothing mythical about the centenarians growing old not in distress but in pure grace.

Among the popular regions that are believed to host the healthiest and happiest elder population, **Abkhazia** in the Caucasus, Southern Russia stands out. According to an article written by John Robbins, Dr. Leaf did not only interview and observe the people there. He took their blood pressure, examined their heartbeat, and studied carefully how they go about their everyday lives. In the end, Dr. Leaf was left in awe. He met men and women way past 100, not looking their age. They can climb the mountains swiftly and can walk through long distances without a sweat; they continue to work and perform even challenging duties; they have sharp memories, superb vision, and excellent hearing.

After Dr. Leaf published his articles about the long life in Abkhazia, controversy started brewing swiftly. They say that the age claims are difficult to believe. When birth records are not present, it is difficult for a good number of observers to just trust what Dr. Leaf claims.

On top of that, there were companies and manufacturers who took advantage of the supposed findings and used them for their business interests. There are yoghurt companies, in fact, that used the Abkhazians to promote their product in American market. Many of them succeeded. As the Western population grew interest on achieving the same brand of longevity that the Abkhazians enjoy, they bit into whatever is presented in their plates.

It's Not a Matter of How Old They Are But How They Live!: For John Robbins, however, it is no longer important whether Dr. Leaf can prove that his subjects actually went past 120. As a longstanding fan of longevity, he is content with the facts presented showing off how the elders in those cultures aged in beauty. They are happy and cheerful and charming and healthy. Not many people past young age can joke around and move around with ease. For that alone, Robbins like to believe that the Abkhazian lifestyle is truly remarkable.

The Quest for the Secret to Happy and Healthy Aging Continues. In our modern world, it is quite obvious that people continue to search for the true secret of ageless beauty and grace. Science never stops suggesting ways and means to achieve longevity.

If we try to learn through the Abkhazian lifestyle, growing old in beauty is simple. You just need to take on a diet that will not populate your body with toxins, move more frequently with routines that you enjoy, laugh around, and strengthen your personal relationships.

Similarly, there are some other places, where the average life span of the inhabitants is 85-100 years! Another mystery of Nature. Let's look at the facts and figures regarding this riddle.

In **Italy**, on top of the mountain range between Sienna and Naples, there is a village named **Campodimele**. The natural beauty of this village is picturesque, blissful and stunning. In Europe, this village is also known as "Forever Young" village. All of the residents of this village have seen a minimum of 85 years. To uncover the mystery behind the long life of these villagers, a group of European psychologists went to Campodimele and carried out research on them. They found that the villagers live a peaceful and stress free life. Their eating habits are vegetarian and controlled. Their diet is mandated by fresh fruits, green vegetables, milk, sprouts and boiled cereals. They relax for a time after lunch. Traditionally, they sleep by the early evening and wake up fairly early in the morning. They spend their life in the proximity of Mother Nature.

Nature's comparable gift has been given to the people of **Symi** island of **Greece**. The average age of the inhabitants here is 90 years. All residents use tomato, vegetables and salad in abundance. Normally they eat raw or less than cooked vegetables. Due to their diet or nature's unique gift, these people are found working very hard even at the age of 80-90. Hard work, integrity and goodwill are the basis of this society. Their family life is bonded with strong threads of mutual love and caring with a supportive and charitable nature. Inhabitants of this island live stress-free and happy lives with their families.

In the East China Sea, there is an island group known as **Okinawa** Archipelago. This island is also blessed with longevity. It has been found that the vegetables like sweet potato, leafy vegetables, and cereals are part of their daily diet. Soya bean also forms an essential part of their diet. According to the physiologists, all these elements contain antioxidants, which stop the harmful effects of aging and growth of cancerous free radical cells. Significantly their food contains minimal salt, as a result these people don't have blood pressure and heart related diseases. Even at the age of 80, they can easily do farming. They are very fond of exercises such as, gardening, walking, folk dance and ancient marshal arts. Inhabitants of Okinawa give a great deal of importance to **meditation**. They successfully try to resolve all of their problems through meditation.

Much research and many tests have been conducted to understand the secret behind the longevity of inhabitants of different regions but no conclusive outcome has been achieved. One thing is for sure that by leading life in a balanced, harmonious, mutually loving, self-controlled and systematic manner and in companionship with nature, one can attain good health and longevity. Naturalists have also come to a consensus that nature and life have a deep inter-connection.

It is believed that in ancient India average age of a person used to be 100 years. Ayurvedic scriptures provide an answer to this. They profess to follow the regimen of *Hitbhuk, Ritbhuk and Mitbhuk* to attain long and healthy life. *Hitbhuk* means eating according to the state of health and what is beneficial for health. Eat for health and not taste. *Ritbhuk* means eat food according to the season and that is prepared with goodwill. *Mitbhuk* means eat with moderation. Don't overeat. People desirous of attaining healthy body and healthy mind should strictly follow this advice.

Brief Summary of the Secrets of Centenarians

What are the longevity secrets of these super centenarians and how can they help you reach your goals of a long and fulfilling lifetime?

1. Eat Well: Super centenarians eat simply and many eat a colorful plate that includes lots of fruits and vegetables. Green leafy vegetables, red tomatoes rich in lycopene, dark colored fruits such as blueberries, plenty of fiber and oily fish will go a long way toward giving you a well rounded diet. If you can't get fresh vegetables and fruits, eat them frozen since they are usually preserved at the moment of their peak freshness, which is when they are the most nutritious.

Needless to say, it's better to leave off foods high in fats, salt, and calories and only eat a little red meat per week.

2. Exercise: Centenarians are generally active now or were very active in their younger years. Experts believe any kind of exercise, no matter how simple, is better than not doing anything and you're never too old to get started.

Climb Stairs- running up and down a flight of stairs five times a day is actually good for most people, contrary to popular thought.

Walking- walk briskly for 30 minutes three times per week.

Lift Weights- Experts believe bone and muscle loss can be stopped, and in some cases, reversed by lifting weights. Recently, a group of women in their 50's and 60's were able to score as well as women in their 30's on a strength test after a weight lifting program.

3. Social: Keep a strong social network of friends. Make friends by becoming indispensable to others. That can mean doing a lot of favors and being considerate. Naturally, most people will reciprocate but building up social credit is not the biggest pay-off. You have a deep need to feel needed. That gives you purpose and rounds out the rough areas of your life. It will also make you happy.

4. Curiosity: Stay interested in your world and increase your surroundings, instead of cocooning inside yourself. That may mean reading, surfing on The Internet, or just going out any chance you get. I know of one lady who will be 101 on her next birthday and she is a member of the Red Hat Club. She's a doer and gets on the bus with the others anytime they go out. In fact, she has very little patience with seniors up to twenty years her junior who spend most of their time complaining and watching television.

5. Play: Give yourself time to pursue hobbies and pastimes that give you pleasure. Many adults neglect this area of their lives because they think play is only for children. If you like to play the piano, for example, learn a new piece and make sure it is a little difficult. If you want to paint, take art lessons and learn how. Working in your yard may be something you like to do or you may enjoy golf or playing chess or bridge. If you don't have a hobby, find one so you won't be dependent on others to entertain you as you get older.

6. Sleep: Most Americans do not get enough sleep, or they can't sleep well. Doctors still think 7 to 8 hours of sleep per night is a good rest period and should be consistent with a schedule you stick to, even on weekends. Refrain from eating and drinking up to two hours before bedtime. Do not exercise within three hours before retiring. A work-out stimulates you and does not help you settle down for a good restful sleep. Also, check your mattress for sturdiness and comfort, if you're having trouble sleeping. Surprisingly it could be causing some sleeping problems.

7. Goals: Don't give up on your goal to become a centenarian. Even people with chronic conditions such as heart disease, diabetes, and high blood pressure are living to 100. Good genes certainly help and people in bad health can't expect miracles, but more and more people are controlling their chronic conditions very well. That's because doctors are learning more about how to monitor these conditions and people are taking more of a pro-active approach toward their own health.

It's never too late to start building your life and health around the secrets of super centenarians who have lived to be 100. As geriatric expert, Dr. Thomas Perls states, " the older you get, the healthier you've been." Start now and make one small step toward a successful old age.

Let us look at another study on the affect of life style on life span. For a number of years the Foundation for Optimal Health and Longevity in Bonita, California has engaged in research on why some individuals and population groups are able to maintain vigor of mind and body with advancing age, whereas the majority of individuals follow a course of progressive deterioration. Foundation studies have been done in Ecuador, the Caucuses, Hunzaland, and California.

Population groups in Ecuador, Hunzaland, and the Caucuses were chosen because they have a reputation for being exceptionally long-lived. In Ecuador, Hunzaland and the Caucuses, documentation was lacking. Nonetheless, it seemed clear that there were large numbers of older individuals (over 75) who were exceptionally vigorous in body and mind.

The long-lived people in the three population groups cited above had several characteristics in common:

1. They engaged in many hours of physical exertion daily, primarily farming, using hand tools. The work involved much up and downhill walking, and in addition, they frequently carried heavy objects.

2. The diet was, in general, much lower in calories, protein, animal (saturated) fats, cholesterol, and salt, but higher in rough carbohydrates and fiber than the usual American diet.

3. They were generally slender, well muscled, and had a vigorous, youthful appearance.

4. Blood cholesterol levels (106 to 192 mg%) of the Ecuadorian group were much lower than the average healthy American of similar age (150 to 300 mg%).

5. High blood pressure and cardiovascular diseases were virtually non-existent.

6. There was general expectation of living to 100 or more years. Continuing, useful participation in the social and economic life of the community and the family was the usual custom. Indeed, the very old members of the community enjoyed great respect and prestige because of their age and experience.

The second set of studies in the San Diego area were done on two groups of individuals: (1) Highly conditioned men between the ages of 15 and 75 who were long-distance runners and who trained and competed regularly over distances of 1 to 26 miles; and (2) a variety of unconditioned, but normal individuals: schoolgirls and boys ages 9 to 10, individual men and women aged 17 to 69, and firemen and policemen aged 30 to 50. These groups were tested before and after 6 to 12 months of a special exercise and diet program.

The research studies cited above led to the following conclusions:

1. Daily, prolonged physical activity as a part of an individual's lifestyle is a major factor in the maintenance of physical and mental vigor many years beyond the usual retirement age.

2. A diet substantially lower in animal fat, cholesterol, salt, protein, sugar and calories than is present in the typical American diet, is an important factor in the prevention of atherosclerosis (hardening of the arteries) and cardiovascular diseases, and thereby favors an increased life span.

3. The older distance runners in San Diego exhibited physical and blood chemical characteristics similar to those of the long-lived population groups in Ecuador, Hunzaland and the Caucuses. Furthermore, they maintained high physical and mental vigor, showed a low incidence of hypertension and cardiovascular diseases, and had low blood cholesterol and triglyceride levels. They also resembled the long-lived people in body build.

4. Mental and physical deterioration so commonly seen in older individuals in the U.S. is not part of the normal aging process, and therefore avoidable. Deterioration is due to specific diseases or the result of many years of insufficient use of mental and physical abilities. The principal law of aging is that--any function, skill, or tissue that is not used continuously will gradually be lost.

5. Properly designed and supervised exercise programs based on endurance activities appear to be equivalent to the physical activities that are a part of the lifestyle of the long-lived population groups. Such programs, combined with optimal diets, have been successfully used by the Foundation on unconditioned individuals aged 9 to 70 to achieve the physical and biochemical characteristics of the long-lived population groups. These programs are applicable to individuals of all ages.

6. A survey of people over 100 (Parade, October 16, 1988) showed that besides genetic propensity and physical activity, centenarians share characteristics such as:

(1) **Discipline**--set standards and achieve them.

(2) **Altruism**--not self-centered but people-oriented.

(3) **Optimism**--continue to make plans for the future.

(4) **Spiritual faith**--even extra body experience that nothing can really harm and living without fear.

(5) **Love of life**--enjoy simple pleasures with unashamed enthusiasm.

ADDITIONAL TIPS TO MAINTAIN HEALTHY LIFESTYLE

Most of these tips are suggested to help by influencing melatonin levels (discussed later in Chapter 8). Melatonin is believed to be nature's age-reversing, disease fighting, health-enhancing, cycle restoring hormone.

1. A lifestyle that follows predictable routines will make it easier for your body to maintain its proper function. Keep your schedule, such as sleeping and waking, synchronized with your body's basic rhythms.

2. Humans have evolved in a world governed by the sun. Many health problems, including depression, sleeplessness, and such physical manifestations of stress as heart disease and high blood pressure may be brought about by our lack of exposure to sunlight. So keep in touch with the nature's gift of sunlight.

3. If you feel that your body is rebelling against the way you live, listen to it--whether it's losing weight or quitting smoking. In fact, by making minor lifestyle changes now, you can prevent the kinds of problems--high blood pressure, for example, that will require much more radical changes later on.

4. Sleepiness during the day, like sleeplessness at night, suggests that your basic circadian rhythms may be out of sync. In addition, it may

be a sign of depression. Incorporate lifestyle changes to follow your body's natural sleep-wake patterns to get more restful sleep.

5. If you notice signs of aging (for example, trouble sleeping or reduced resistance to disease), this is an indication that you should follow the lifestyle changes that can help delay these and other signs of aging as suggested throughout this guide.

6. To handle depression--especially when it comes and goes with the seasons--ask your doctor about phototherapy as part of your treatment. Increasing your exposure to light can help overcome seasonal changes in mood.

7. Fresh fruits, fresh vegetables, fresh air, plenty of sunlight--that's a diet just about anyone can add to one's lifestyle.

8. Protect yourself from environmental factors such as pollution and exposure to electric fields.

Additional common sense practices to slow down aging are discussed in the next chapter.

Chapter 4

COMMON SENSE TIPS TO SLOW AGING

As we have learned, none of the age-related findings present an immediate solution to slow down the aging process---not yet at least. At this time, it is difficult to practice any particular method for slowing down the process of aging. Hints based on experimental evidence of certain theories, as well as on common sense ideas, are presented below and they may be used to supplement the overall health approach.

Vitamin E and C

The free radical-oxidation theory of aging would suggest the use of antioxidants to slow down the damaging processes in the cells of body, caused by free radicals and oxidation. Using Vitamin E in order to feel young is a familiar idea to most of us. Since vitamin E and vitamin C are antioxidants, the theory would suggest that a simple and safe, practice to slow free radical and oxidation related damage would be to take vitamin E and C regularly. Vitamin E (oil soluble) primarily protects cell membranes and vitamin C (water soluble) protects the inside part of the cell, in its watery fluid. How much of these vitamins should be taken daily to slow down aging is an open question. The amounts of these vitamins used by Dr. Linus Pauling (Nobel Laureate in Chemistry and peace) include 2 grams of vitamin C and 1200 units of vitamin E, which are more than thirty times the U.S. recommended daily allowances. However, in the absence of specific data, a lower amount would be safer; not more than 500 mg (half a gram) of vitamin C and 400 units of vitamin E. Too much of an antioxidant can interfere with a cell's oxidation reactions and might impair the cell's functioning in some vital way.

Melatonin (described in detail in Chapter 8), is one of the most powerful *antioxidants* ever discovered. When it is present in cells, it prevents the chemical damage of oxidation from occurring. By blocking cellular oxidation, melatonin may help prevent changes in blood vessels that lead to hypertension and heart attacks, and may reduce the likelihood of certain kinds of cancer. Regular doses may range from half a milligram to 5 milligram per day as discussed in Chapter 8.

Selenium, present in trace amounts in a wide variety of foods, seems to have an important antioxidant role, although it is not tested in humans. Other antioxidants such as BHT (used by the food industry to preserve freshness of stored foods) and ethxyquin have been shown to prolong the life of laboratory animals up to 25 percent higher than average. However, these at present are not considered safe for human consumption in amounts proportional to those used in animal experiments. Still, they offer support to the general theory that the use of antioxidants may serve as a possible method for life extension.

Lowering Polyunsaturated Fats in the Diet

Polyunsaturated fat (vegetable oils) is one of the substances which is more easily oxidized than others and thus gives rise to more free radical reactions, presumably, therefore, promoting aging due to free radical mediated damage to cells. Polyunsaturated fats have long been recommended as a replacement for saturated fats in order to reduce cholesterol in the blood, yet according to Dr. Harman of the University of Nebraska College of Medicine, all dietary fat, not just saturated fat, should be limited. He found that increased amounts of polyunsaturated fats in the diet of mice decreased their life span, which he hypothesized was due to increased levels of free radical reactions. Moreover, two of five dietary regimes substituting vegetable oil for butter and animal fats have shown an increase in cancer in humans. Drs. Gabriel Fernandes and Robert Good, formerly of Sloan-Kettering cancer center have shown that in mice, several types of cancer are increased by diets high in polyunsaturated fats. At this point, the lesson is that a lower intake of fat, whether saturated or unsaturated, is nutritionally healthful. For fat lovers, monounsaturated fats such as from olive oil, walnuts, and flex seeds are the best.

Dieting to Slow Aging

One of the life-lengthening effects of dietary restriction (see Calorie Restriction in Chapter 2), according to Dr. Roy Walford of UCLA, is due to its slowing the rate of autoimmune aging. As discussed earlier, during age-related development of autoimmunity, the body fails to recognize its own cells and attacks and damages them. The prolongation of life induced by dietary restriction, Walford claims, is due to the fact that the immune system is more susceptible than any other body system to starvation. Dietary restriction does not seem to harm the immune system; instead it slows its harmful effect of attacking the body's own cells.

Another explanation of why dieting slows aging is that melatonin production increases in the digestive tract when calories are restricted. Melatonin being an age-reversing hormone increases the life span (see Chapter 8 on Melatonin and Aging). Just as the eyes gauge light and dark, regulating the pineal's production of melatonin, so does the digestive system gauge food supplies, adjusting melatonin levels in response. In addition, this theory may offer some insight into why "lifestyle" diseases such as heart disease and cancer so often seem to be associated with rising prosperity--when melatonin production decreases in the digestive tract due to an abundant supply of calories.

In any case, restricting our diets by eating less, but maintaining adequate amounts of nutrition is healthy and can thus increase the life expectancy. The statistical data also supports that average or lower body weight up to 20 pounds increases the life expectancy as compared to overweight, and the restriction of diet in rats has been shown to increase their life spans up to 25 percent. The beneficial effects of lower weight to reduce the chances of heart diseases as well as the chances of diabetes, nephritis, cerebral hemorrhage, and various diseases of the digestive system are fairly well known.

Vital statistics show that thin people live longer than those who are overweight (see Table 4.1). A moderate degree of underweight is advantageous. Consequently, those who wish a long and healthy life should keep their weight slightly below, rather than at, the average level for age, height, and body build. Overweight, on the other hand, is disadvantageous, with excess mortality roughly proportional to the degree of overweight. Only 60 percent of obese people (20 % or more overweight) reach the age of 60, compared with 90 percent of slim persons. Thirty percent of the obese reach the age of 70, while 50 percent of the slim reach 70. The age of 80 is reached by only 10 percent of the obese, compared with 30 percent of the thin, a ratio of one to three. The effects of overweight on mortality show that overweight is associated with excessive mortality (as mentioned above) from heart disease, diabetes, nephritis, cerebral hemorrhage, and various diseases of the digestive system. Overweight people have difficulties with their feet and back because of the added burden of weight on the skeleton, and have, as well an increased incidence of gout and arthritis. They suffer from shortness of breath, especially on exertion and face increased risk of surgery.

Table 4.1 Mortality of men in different weight classes.

Weight Class		Percent decrease or increase over normal death rate*					
		Age under 40			Age 40 and over		
		Short men	Medium men	Tall men	Short men	Medium men	Tall men
Underweight: Below Average							
40 lb	18 kg	15	15	--	20	0	0
20 lb	9 kg	-5	-10	-10	0	-5	-5
Average Weight:		0	0	0	0	0	0
Overweight: Above average							
20 lb	9 kg	15	10	10	20	20	10
40 lb	18 kg	35	25	25	35	30	25
60 lb	27 kg	90	45	45	60	50	45

*For example, 20 lb above average weight for short men under age 40 increase chances of death by 15 %, whereas 20 lb below average decrease by 5 % over normal death rate.

SOURCE: Based on Build and Blood Pressure Study, Society of Actuaries, Chicago.

Nucleic Acid Therapy

The genetic theory of nucleic acid damage with age gives rise to the suggestion that a diet rich in nucleic acids can not only prevent but also repair such damage. This might make cells function as efficiently as cells in younger individuals. Dr. Benjamin Frank of New York has claimed recovery of his patients from degenerative diseases by keeping them on a diet which was rich in DNA and RNA content. Although this is as yet quite speculative, there is definitely no harm in using this therapy and we can make a routine habit of eating foods which provide one to one and a half grams of nucleic acids per day. Patients with gout disease should, however, be careful because they cannot metabolize the amounts of purines provided by such a diet.

Since nucleic acids as such are not studied as nutrients, nutritionists do not have data on nucleic acid contents of foods. Perhaps findings such as those mentioned above may lead to more nutritional studies being directed towards this approach. Based on various sources, some general guidelines for a choice of foods rich in nucleic acids are provided below. You are probably accustomed to most of the foods. The proper distribution of these foods in a weekly diet would provide an average daily intake of one to two grams of nucleic acids in dietary form. Among meats, food sources of nucleic acids include sardines, salmon, non-vertebrate seafood (such as shrimp, lobster, clams, oysters), any kind of fish, and liver meats (e.g. chicken liver, beef liver). As pointed out above, a diet high in meat, especially the ones containing higher amounts of nucleic acids, is believed to raise the uric acid level associated with gout disease. Therefore, plenty of fluids including water and fruit or vegetable juices should be used with a nucleic acid diet. Foods more appropriate to vegetarian diets, such as pinto and other beans, lentils, peas, asparagus, mushrooms, and spinach, are high in nucleic acids and should be included in the daily diet in accordance with individual eating habits. Vegetarian foods are also low in fat and cholesterol, and as compared to meats, the danger of increase in uric acid level is also low. The germinating seeds of soybeans, for example, can provide about twice the amounts of nucleic acids as compared to dry seeds containing the same nutritional value. Thus, sprouts which are generally associated with health foods are a good source of nucleic acids. As a rule of thumb, actively growing plant parts--in which cells are dividing and therefore DNA is being synthesized--are high in nucleic acids.

Some Common Healthy Activities to Slow Aging

Researchers in the field of gerontology support the positive effect of the following life activities on our health and aging.

1.   Since a high stress environment is dangerous to health and longevity, the practice of mental approaches to reduce stress are the cost effective and safe way to control stress, and have been proven effective for centuries.

2.   An active life---having a reason for living---can prolong life. We know that people who are young have eager, inquisitive minds. They are curious, always seeking and evaluating answers. They are willing to try something new--a new approach to a job, a new kind of music, a new response to a recurring situation.

3.   An active sex life, in general, is suggested to prolong youthful health. In healthy old men, the sex hormone testosterone has been observed at levels similar to those of younger men and sexual activity is related to hormonal level. Which comes first---the hormone level or active sex life---researchers have yet to determine. Observations on people over sixty have indicated that men and women do not lose their physical capacity for sexual performance in terms of erection and orgasm; and sex experts believe that sexual activity helps to preserve sexual functioning and youthful feelings.

4.   Good marriage and social life can prolong life. For example, married couples live longer than single people with an otherwise similar social life. These effects may be due in part to reduced stress as compared to lonely people.

5.   Mental exercises such as reading and crossword puzzles, and physical aerobic exercises for about 15 minutes, three times a week can go a long way towards preserving the body and mind. However, exertion can actually shorten lifespan. So the message is to *do* but don't *overdo.*
Note: Between 1930-1960 the medical profession regarded vigorous exercise as a form of stress that would wear out the body. We know now that in contrast to machines which wear out with use, human

organs and tissues develop an adaptive increase in function with use that runs counter to the changes which occur in aging.

6.   Seven guidelines, some of which are familiar to us, have been suggested by various health experts to prolong life. These include no smoking, moderate weight, moderate drinking, physical activity, eating breakfast, regular meals, and sleeping seven or eight hours-- but not less than six or more than nine.

In the overall conclusion, safe habits to prolong life include proper nutrition, a diet rich in fiber, and low in animal fat, sugar and refined foods. Certain aging theories suggest a possible role of vitamin E and C and foods rich in nucleic acids as another nutritional aspect of long and healthy living. However, some of the ideas of the eastern world such as yogic breathing for vigor and vitality, postures to keep youthful body flexibility, and the effect of mind on our health and performance, are very important for healthy and youthful living. These ideas of the eastern world that are based on centuries of experience, are certainly safe and effective as compared to the modern aging theories which are still in the exploration stage.

New Approaches to Slow Aging

While getting old is nobody's favorite topic, but the way we think about aging can actually affect our biological age. We should learn to appreciate what is being gained by the wisdom of experience. The biological markers of aging like blood pressure, bone density, body temperature regulation, immune functions, skin thickness, wrinkles, fat content, cardiovascular function, and many other markers of aging are actually quite changeable according to the circumstance. Some modifications in our attitude can go long way to slow aging.

On Flexibility: Flexibility is a critical component of lifelong good health. A healthy body is a flexible body. Cultivating a flexible consciousness is an important underlying aspect of physical health, that if we're rigid in our consciousness that will express its rigidity in our body because the mind and body are inseparable. In addition to physical disciplines like yoga, the ability to let go of our rigid attachments to a specific outcome is one of the healthiest things we can do.

The Power of Love: What could be more potent than the power of love? People say love heals all wounds, but how it does that is a real mystery. Most people think of love as an emotional sentiment, but that it's much more than that. Love is the knowingness and the experience of inseparability of us as one being. Love has also been shown to restore homeostasis, which is the body's natural inclination toward balance and healing.

The Power of Intention: Intention is one of the most powerful forces in the universe. We can focus on that power in keeping ourselves healthy. If we want to heal ourselves then first of all we have to have clarity of what our intended outcome is. Then, when we have clarity of that intended outcome in consciousness, we can enter into the field of silence (such as meditation) so that the intention orchestrates its own fulfillment.

Releasing Negative Energy: Toxic feelings like anger and resentment are more than just unpleasant; they can actually be dangerous to our health. Toxic emotions at the molecular level are as damaging as any other toxin. In order to deal with these emotions, we must take responsibility for our own emotions, witness the emotion in our body, label it, and express it in non-toxic ways such as journaling or therapy. The all-important final step is to then release the toxic emotion, to let it go, and share your emotional victory with someone you love who understands you.

The Miracle of Nature: Nature provides us with healing substances in abundance, if we know how to use them. Nature also provides us with information, if we're paying attention. We can learn about how a caterpillar transforms into a butterfly, and how this process represents a "quantum leap of creativity in nature" that we can also achieve ourselves, personally and socially, through the power of intention.

Our Shadow Side: Every human being has a shadow; if you don't have a shadow it means you're not standing in the light. The shadow is the part of ourselves that we might be embarrassed by, that we might be ashamed of, that we don't want other people to find out about -- but that we should embrace our shadow, forgive our shadow and, most importantly, share our shadow with somebody we trust.

On Cells in Alignment: The intricate life of our cells is truly amazing. In fact, our cells have a lot to teach us about living a spiritual life. Every cell in our body is aware of what's happening in the rest of the body. Every cell has acceptance. Every cell communes with every other cell and has a memory of wholeness. Turns out this is what living a spiritual life is all about.

The Law of Least Effort: We in our culture have become brainwashed to believe that hard work, exacting plans and driving ambition is the way to succeed. While it might be, by the time you get what you want you may also have high blood pressure, you're addicted to drugs and your children have joined a gang. By not always looking for a response about the future, or regretting the past, we accept the present moment and the Universe begins providing us what we want – with minimal effort. Remember: **"Nobody can go back and start a new beginning, but anyone can start today and make a new ending."**

On Meditation: We hear a lot about the benefits of meditation, but many of us have a hard time doing it. The best approach is to have no expectations when meditating, to avoid thinking there's a right way or wrong way to do it. We begin our meditation practice by just learning to sit for 15 or 20 minutes and simply experience whatever we feel, including the restlessness and all the body sensations. In fact, learning to feel into our emotions and body sensations is great pathway into meditation!

Listening to Our Bodies: The best way to teach our body to be healthy, is actually to listen to it. Our body's biological rhythms are the symphony of the whole Universe. Just as our planet, our bodies have circadian, seasonal, lunar and gravitational rhythms. A body that is healthy is tuned into these rhythms, which requires us to listen to our bodies as a microcosm of the cosmic body.

Yoga for Health: Yoga is an important part of many of our lives these days. It's a great way to get physical exercise, but it can also have much more profound significance. The deeper meaning of yoga is "union with source" or with the ultimate spirit. Yoga postures facilitate mind-body coordination and mind-body synthesis, and bring about a natural balance in our bodies called homeostasis.

On Ancestors: Knowing our ancestors is really the activation of archetypal energies embodied in the mythologies of our culture. Archetypes are states of consciousness, and if we tap into them, then that state of consciousness directly affects our behaviors. Inviting these states of consciousness to incarnate through us, we start to interact with people and look at the world in a different way, one that taps into our collective imagination.

The Biology of Belief: It's important that patients believe the diagnosis from their doctor because if they don't, and the diagnosis has been made accurately, then they're not going to get the right treatment. But believing in the diagnosis is not the same as believing in the prognosis, because the prognosis of a disease does not tell you about the outcome of that disease in a particular person. Our beliefs have a powerful impact on our health outcomes and should not be overlooked.

The Healing Power of Laughter: As you might expect, the tears of laughter have a completely different chemistry than the tears of sorrow. You can't be experiencing laughter and have your ego in the same way at the same time because the molecules of emotion secreted from laughter are very different than the molecules you experience in ordinary or depressed states of consciousness. These molecules of emotion, called neuropeptides, have even been shown to affect the activity of the immune system in a healthy direction.

Dealing With Addiction: Addiction is the number one disease of our civilization, addiction to toxic behavior, toxic substances, toxic relationships, toxic environment – which all create a toxic body. Ayurveda sees addiction as a second-class substitute for the exultation of the spirit. The most powerful approach is to actually give the person a sense of higher ecstasy and pleasure than the one they remember from the addictive substance.

The Keys to a Joyful Long Life: People think that if they had the right relationship they'd be joyful. If they had enough money, if they were in good health, then they'd be joyful. It's actually the other way around. If we're happy to begin with, then we're more likely to be healthy and make healthy choices, and we're likely to have the right relationships and more likely to be successful because we come from a place of strength.

Some Interesting Prescriptions to Slow Aging

The search for a way to restore youth and vigor and to extend life is man's oldest quest, the mystery that has tantalized him for centuries. Egyptians and Romans ate garlic in large quantities to lengthen life and increase strength. Many early Europeans tried youth-regaining remedies such as roots of the mandrake plant (belonging to the potato family) and even insects such as the Spanish fly.

Among the most popular youth-regaining remedies were the transplants or extracts of healthy sexual organs of animals such as monkey and goat testicles as a form of rejuvenation therapy. The rejuvenation therapy by injecting with cells from fetal animals was pioneered by a Swiss Doctor Paul Niehans who made a fortune by treating wealthy and often famous senior citizens. Among other remedies are, the lowering of body temperature in certain experimental animals to slow aging. Shots of the anesthetic procaine called *Gerovital* (made up of procaine hydrochloride and haematoporphyrin) has been claimed to help elderly patients regain youthful characteristics such as improved memory, muscular strength and skin texture. Still other suggestions that have been made to slow down aging are hormone preparations, lipofuscin inhibitors, lysosome membrane stabilizers and cross-link inhibitors. However, the use of the above youth-promoting techniques in the absence of data and scientific validity; are extremely dangerous, even if you ignore the possibility of long term side effects. Clearly, getting the right food into our bodies along with moderate adherence to safe health practices and mental tranquility which are backed up by some scientific validity is a good start towards health and longevity.

Chapter 5

BREATHING AND LONGEVITY

You're never too old to start yoga and breathing. Hazel, a centenarian, is in such great shape, both physically and mentally, she wanted to mark this milestone, and a huge party was thrown in her honor on 100th birthday. While celebrating the 100th birthday party, at that point, his great grand daughter Jane, a yoga teacher asked, "What do you think the secret to your longevity is grand ma?"

Hazel thought for a moment, and then said "Oh, it's the yoga and breathing, it's definitely the yoga."

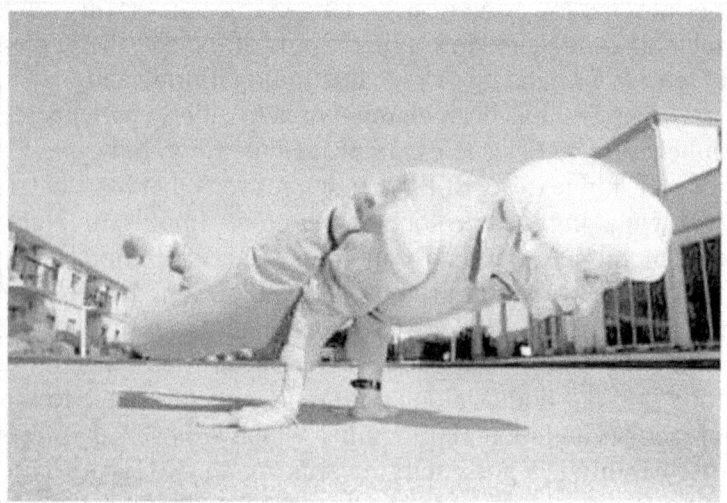

Jane was shocked. Jane has taught yoga for more than ten years, and had never heard her grand ma mention yoga to her. Grand ma continued to explain wisely how you have to do one side, and then the other. And you have to do it reeeaaal slow. And you have to have a good yoga teacher, "like my Jane over here." (This made Jane smile.)

Then Jane asked, "So, exactly how long have you been doing yoga?"

Grand ma Hazel replied "Oh... about 6 months now."

I love this story. You are never too old to start a yoga practice!

In this chapter we will emphasize, an important but ignored aspect of longevity, which is healthful breathing and its relationship with aging. The importance of breathing for longevity goes back to the 18th century as offered in an eighteenth-century treatise entitled, *"Hermippus Redividicus,* or the Sage's Triumph over Old Age and the Grave, wherein a method is laid down for prolonging the vigor of man, including a commentary upon an ancient inscription, in which this great secret is revealed, supported by numerous authorities." A man aged, according to the treatise, because he lost vital particles every time he exhaled. The great secret--how to find a new source of particles--was revealed by the discovery of a tomb whose occupant had reportedly lived to the age of 115. The fellow managed to live so long, according to the tomb's inscription, with the aid of the breath of young women. Today, even though we are not looking for exhaled vital particles, but experts advice aerobics and breathing exercises, and gerontologists are measuring vital capacities to see how well our lungs can maintain the exchange of oxygen and carbon dioxide as we age.

Changes in Respiration During the Life Span

During the various stages of life, boys and girls follow distinct courses in the development of their respective breathing patterns. Among children ranging in age from seven to fourteen, boys in general tend to have a more highly developed lung function than girls of equivalent age. For instance, girls nine to eleven years of age normally tend to have a respiratory capacity which is 10 percent less than that of boys in the same age group. By the age of twelve, the difference between boys' and girls' respective respiratory capacity widens to an average of 20 percent. This difference persists until the age of fourteen. Researchers attribute the large differences between girls and boys, principally, to the internal secretion of sex hormones, especially, testosterone, a male sex hormone believed to play a key role in promoting muscle development and consequently, respiratory capacity among boys.

The general respiratory capacity of men improves constantly through late adolescence, until the age of between eighteen and twenty. After that period, however, capacity decreases gradually from year to year.

By way of example, using the average figure for eighteen to twenty year-olds as an index of 100, average respiratory capacity declines as shown in Table 5.1.

Table 5.1. Changes in respiratory capacity by age.

Age (years)	Respiratory Capacity (% of Maximum)
18-20	100.00
20-23	95.90
32-34	90.17
41-43	86.07
51- 53	81.86
56-60	76.36
61-65	67.38
71-75	60.48
75-80	56.24

After reaching a peak during the early part of life, between the ages of eighteen and twenty, the symptoms of respiratory senility seem to manifest themselves in men during their late forties. In women, these signs tend to appear some ten years earlier than in men. It happens that the appearance of these signs seem to coincide with the appearance of the signs of aging in the muscle tissue of the human body. It is therefore, most important for middle-aged people to master the techniques necessary to maintain respiratory capacity for as long as possible.

The most effective way to prevent the exacerbation of aging phenomena is for a person to learn how to maintain a regular respiration cycle and to rejuvenate himself by taking regular breathing cycles. This way of exercise can be more useful to rejuvenate than outdoor exercises like jogging and track and field athletics which many people undertake for the purpose of wearing off surplus fat.

Decreased Lung Function With Age

A decrease in lung volume has been the most frequently observed influence of aging. The rigidity of the rib cage contributes to lung volume decrease from 40 percent of the total in young individuals to 30 percent of the total by 80 years of age. The lung volume alterations influence flow rate, such as voluntary ventilation, expiratory flow rate and forced expiratory volume. Among other parameters, maximal oxygen uptake peaks at age 20 and then declines with increasing age. Past 40 years of age the basal metabolic rate (oxygen consumption) slowly declines until about 80 years of age when a very rapid decline is noted.

Decreased lung capacity and chest expansion reflect forced vital capacity (FVC) and determine the volume of air one can expel after taking a deep breath. The vital capacity which is independent of sex, weight, and smoking habits appears to decline steadily with age in both sexes. The average decline in vital capacity over the years is given in Table 5.2.

Table 5.2. Changes in vital capacity (total air moved in and out of lungs) by age.

Age (year)	Vital Capacity (ml)
30	5,000
40	4,500
50	3,750
60	3,000
70	2,500

According to the American Lung Association, a healthy man's lung function peaks when he is about 25 (a woman's normally peaks at around 20), then begins a gradual decline. The decline according to the American Lung Association that averages about one percent per year, is not noticeable, and barring illness, lungs will serve well as long as one lives. However, studies have associated decline in lung capacity with decreased longevity and, therefore, it is important to maintain lung function. Dr. Kenneth Cooper, who is credited with starting the worldwide jogging craze, suggests that the vital capacity need not fall off with age if one does aerobic exercises. According to Dr. Michael Pollock--a prominent exercise physiologist, highly motivated, highly trained, and well-conditioned distance runners have staved off an expected decline in lung and heart function over at least a ten-year-span. For example, Pollock's study at Mount Sinai Medical Centre in Milwaukee showed that Hal Higdon, a runner, had maximum intake of oxygen during vigorous exercise (VO2 max) ranging 62.7, 69.4 and 63.2 at ages of 41, 46 and 51, respectively. To even the most skeptical observer, these numbers do not indicate any decline. Rather they represent a gain in one aging man's capacity to extract and use oxygen in middle age. Even if you are not a runner, aerobic workouts and breathing exercises tend to increase the capacity of the lungs, which is associated with greater longevity.

The reasons for decline in vital capacity with age are not clear, but it seems to be related more to chest wall function than to intrinsic factors in the lung function. Other indicators related to decline in breathing capacity show that older adults breathe with greater difficulty and less satisfaction than in earlier years.

Breathing exercises (given later in this chapter) improve breathing efficiency, as well as lung capacity and chest expansion. When the breathing pattern is altered so that large tidal volumes are utilized, the age-related problems of breathing efficiency can be significantly reduced. For example, deep breathing would increase lung volume, open closed airways and improve distribution of inspired air. This would tend to support the claims that breathing exercises maintain youthful health and improve vigor and vitality.

Decline in Age-related Heart Rate and Oxygen Delivery

In addition to other factors, such as decreased lung function, the decline in oxygen delivery to cells also results from the poor blood circulation due to age-related decline in heart rate. The decline in maximal heart rate with age is shown in Table 5.3. A rough estimate of maximal heart rate for any age can be obtained by subtracting age in years from 220. For example, for a thirty-five-year-old, the maximal heart rate is 220 minus 35, or 185 beats per minute (training heart rate during an aerobic exercise is determined as 70 to 80% of maximal heart rate). The above equation, where we subtract age, is indicative of steady decline in heart rate with age. So aerobic exercises including breathing techniques provide a good way to keep up the declining circulation and oxygen supply with advancing age.

Table 5.3. Mean maximum heart rate in beats per minute at different ages.

Age (years)	Maximum Heart Rate
25	200
30	194
35	188
40	182
45	176
50	171
55	165
60	159
65	153

SOURCE: Lenore R. Zohman, Beyond Diet: Your Way to Fitness and Health. American Heart Association booklet.

Decreased Respiratory Function of Mitochondria with Age

The production of energy from the food and inhaled oxygen takes place in small cellular organelles called *mitochondria.* Age-related degenerative changes in mitochondrial structure and defects in the respiratory function of the mitochondria have been noted in a number of tissues including brain, muscle and liver of experimental animals. Moreover, several studies have shown an actual decrease in the number of mitochondria with increasing age. In view of the vital metabolic role of mitochondria in providing energy for the cells, this decrease in number of mitochondria as well as degenerative changes are undoubtedly detrimental to the health and even threaten the survival of an individual.

Breathing and aerobic exercises, however, can help to maintain the age-related decrease in number and function of mitochondria (sites of energy production). As we force the cells of our body to produce energy during exercise, the mitochondria are activated to become more efficient and also actually to increase in number. Therefore, breathing and other aerobic exercises combined with proper nutrition increase mitochondrial function and metabolic rate. This increase in metabolic rate not only makes us feel more energetic but also helps to clear fat from the body and maintain proper weight. The maintenance of metabolic rate and body weight are the functions that require special attention as we age; and breathing exercises can help to preserve these functions.

Sleep Variations Due to Age-related Breathing Disturbances

The frequency of sleeplessness that increases with age (Table 1.1, chapter 1), can be largely related to breathing disturbances. These breathing disturbances can be regulated by concentrating on proper breathing.

Researchers have now found that many awakenings are due to breathing disturbances among, healthy, elderly individuals. For regulating the breath to better sleep, lower weight (in addition to learning the proper use of diaphragm and breathing practices) is very helpful; because diaphragm can move freely for efficient breathing. Lying position that interferes with breathing, such as lying on stomach, should be carefully avoided. In this position the body weight prevents the diaphragm and the rib cage from properly expanding. The importance of breathing again comes into the picture for regulating the breath for better sleep in elderly people.

Breathing Exercises to Slow Age-related Changes

As we age and exercise less, our breathing becomes more shallow. Thus over a period of time circulation is gradually decreased. As with other body parts the brain also receives less and less oxygen. The possibility exists that the failure of memory in later years is, at least partly, connected with the undernourishment of the brain cells by oxygen.

Breathing to Keep Brain Cells Healthy:

a.1. Sitting in your chair, exhale completely and bend over. Let your head dangle as close to the floor as possible. Your palms should be touching the floor.

2. Close your eyes and let the blood flow to your head. Stay in this position for a count of fifteen. You may breathe normally while in this position.

3. Slowly lift yourself up and begin to inhale the complete breath.

4. As you reach your normal sitting position, exhale. Repeat if desired.

b.1. Stand up and clasp your hands behind your neck.

2. Inhale the complete breath.

3. Bend forward from the waist and blow the air out from your mouth. The ending should be done quickly. Try to get your head as far down as possible, hopefully touching your knees.

4. Return to your standing position, inhale and repeat ten times.

The above exercises will be helpful to keep your brain cells alive with good supply of oxygenated blood.

Note: Headstand and other upside-down postures like shoulder stand or hanging on a bar using ankle-lock are very important for rich supply of blood to the brain. Daily practice of these exercises for 10 to 15 minutes increases the memory and intellectual power, and slows down the age-related loss of brain cells thus protecting from senility associated with old age. Persons with health conditions like high blood pressure should not attempt upside-down exercises without consulting their physician.

Breathing Exercises to Maintain Lung Function:

The forced vital capacity that determines the volume of air one can expel after taking a deep breath, declines with age (see Table 5.2). The reasons are not clear, but it appears to be related more to chest wall expansion than to intrinsic factors in the lung function. The breathing exercises for chest expansion progressively fill the chest cavity with increasing amounts of air and facilitate deep natural breathing.

a.1. Stand straight with arms at sides and inhale the total breath. Make sure that first your stomach relaxes and bulges out due to dilation of diaphragm and then your chest expands to fill the upper lungs.

2. While holding the breath lift both arms so that they are straight out in front of you at shoulder level. Now move your arms sideways, then forward, and repeat five times while still holding the breath.

3. Drop your arms lifelessly to your sides and exhale energetically through the wide open mouth.

4. Inhale a total breath

5. Repeat this entire procedure three times. When you finish, your lungs get good expansion and will be capable of holding much more air.

b.1. Lie fiat on your back with your mouth closed, hands folded on your stomach, and your knees flexed. Let your shoulders relax and inhale as deeply as you can--to the count of eight. Push your stomach out as you inhale.

2. Hold your breath to the count of four

3. Exhale slowly to the count of eight

4. Repeat this inhale-hold-exhale cycle five times.

These exercises should be done twice a day. These deep-breathing exercises are recommended by the American Lung association for maintaining healthy lungs. They are also good for relieving stress and smoking urge.

The above are selective examples of breathing exercises. Choose the exercises that suit your individual needs and you will realize that breathing practices are not only adding years to your life but also adding life to your years.

Chapter 6

SCIENTIFIC VIEW ABOUT AGING THERAPIES

This chapter will cover various scientific views and recommendations about aging therapies.

Scientific Views on Vitamins and Minerals as antioxidants

The true fountain of youth will involve stopping those pesky free radicals that are wrecking your DNA and cooking your tissues to death. The most popular anti-aging regimen, practiced by millions of Americans, is to pop anti-oxidant vitamin and mineral pills. There is no firm scientific evidence that gobbling down such supplements actually increases life spans. Simon Melov of the Buck Institute for Aging Research notes that the effects of anti-oxidant pills are fairly weak, since most of the nutrients don't get inside the cells where the free radical damage is occurring. Jay Olshansky dismisses megadose vitamin supplements as "a way to make expensive urine."

On the other hand, Olshansky admits that some people can benefit from vitamin supplements. Epidemiological studies show that vitamin E supplements might help 12 percent of the population. The problem is each individual has no way of knowing now whether he or she is part of that 12 percent. Nevertheless, many of us cover our bets by taking supplements anyway.

A recent study conducted by Bruce Ames' team at Berkeley found that lethargic old rats are perked up by l-carnitine and alpha lipoic acid. Their mitochondrial function improves, they become more active, and their memories get better. A company called Juvenon, founded by Ames and others, is testing the supplements in people with the goal of finding an effective human dose.

Meanwhile, Thomas Perls of Harvard is hunting for longevity genes. Perls noticed a decade ago that people who live to be 100 are often in remarkably good shape. Today, he runs the New England Centenarian Project, whose participants must be 100 years old and have siblings who lived to be over 90. By looking at DNA taken from some 600 participants so far, Perls has found that a region on chromosome four appears to help its carriers become healthy geezers.

Perls and his colleagues have formed a company called Centagenetix to narrow the search for the longevity gene. Once it's identified, Centagenetix will try to produce a Methuselah pill that mimics the activity of the proteins made by the longevity gene.

The M.I.T. biologist Leonard Guarente recently showed that nematode worms with more than one copy of a gene called SIR2 live 50 percent longer than normal worms. This may explain why calorie restriction increases life span, because SIR2 slows down gene activity when a cell is being starved. Guarente and Cynthia Kenyon have already identified genes and enzymatic pathways that increase the life spans of invertebrate species. They believe that these same mechanisms will be found in people, giving them targets at which to aim anti-aging drugs. Guarente and Kenyon have created a company called Elixir, which will try to develop such pharmaceuticals.

Eurkarion, a privately held biotech start-up in Massachusetts, is working with the Buck Institute's Melov to test its novel small-molecule anti-oxidant compounds. Melov has genetically engineered mice that don't produce superoxide dismutase, the oxygen-scavenging enzyme that protects mitochondria from free radicals.

Such mice typically die within a week after birth. They suffer from enlarged hearts, damaged livers, and a spongiform brain ailment that looks very much like mad cow disease. But when these mice are injected with compounds that mimic the effects of superoxide dismutase and catalase (a compound that transforms hydrogen peroxide into water), they live four times longer. Eukarion is currently testing one of its compounds as a topical application to heal skin damaged by radiation treatments. It plans to test further compounds as treatments for degenerative neurological diseases in human beings.

As for the gunk built up in our cells, researchers are testing some compounds that break apart AGEs (ADVANCED GLYCATION END PRODUCTS), enabling cells to get rid of them. In preliminary testing, a compound called Pimagedine has improved cardiac function in rats, dogs, and primates. It is also being tested for efficacy in treating kidney failure associated with diabetes. Another anti-AGEing compound, ATL-711, has shown some promise as a treatment to reverse age-related and diabetes-related cardiovascular diseases and restore function to the cardiovascular system.

Runaway Hormones

What about lengthening telomeres? Remember, our immortal germ cells activate the gene that produces the enzyme telomerase, which restores the ends of their telomeres whenever they divide. Cancer cells also stimulate production of the enzyme. The Geron Corporation is conducting research into how to use telomerase to fight cancer. The idea is that if you can turn off telomerase in the cancer cells they will stop dividing and commit cellular suicide, called apoptosis.

Some researchers have suggested that it might be possible to make normal cells immortal by getting them to produce telomerase, which could prevent the shortening of their protective telomeres. It seems logical that if telomere shortening causes cells to become senescent, lengthening them should rejuvenate them and the tissues in which they reside. Still, according to Barbara Hansen, there is little evidence that telomere shortening causes senescence on the organism level.

Hormone replacement therapy is second only to vitamin supplements in popularity among those seeking the fountain of youth. The aim here is to restore the hormones that decline with age to their youthful levels. The most popular hormones involved are DHEA, human growth hormone, melatonin, testosterone, and estrogen.

The notion that hormones could restore youth has a long and disreputable history. In the late 19th century the noted French physiologist Charles Edouard Brown-Sequard injected himself and his patients with extracts from the testicles of young dogs and guinea pigs, then declared that the treatments had restored his physical vigor and mental acuity. In the early 20th century the American John Brinkley claimed to restore men's vitality by transplanting goat testicles into them. He performed over 16,000 transplants before he died, though his medical license was revoked after some of his customers claimed a new compulsion "to chew sprouts."

More recently, hormone replacement therapies took off after the endocrinologist Daniel Rudman reported in 1990 that a dozen older men he had injected with growth hormone three times a week had more muscle mass, less fat, tighter skin, and lower cholesterol levels. Subsequent studies have shown that these quality-of-life benefits are real but slight. In fact, regular exercise is more effective in obtaining most of the gains achieved from injecting growth hormone.

Furthermore, there is no evidence that growth hormone treatments increase longevity. Indeed, mice that overproduce growth hormone die sooner than normal mice, and fruit flies that under-produce growth hormone live longer than normal flies. In addition, some researchers suspect that supplementary growth hormone may increase the risk of cancer.

DHEA is the most abundant steroid in the body, yet nobody knows much about what it does. It is clear that DHEA levels peak in a person's early 20s and decline as he or she ages. Interestingly, feeding DHEA to mice, which produce very small quantities of this hormone naturally, increases their life spans by 40 percent. In *Why We Age*, Steve Austad notes that in the few scientifically valid human trials involving DHEA supplementation, the hormone produced "some improvement in immune response, muscle strength, and sleep patterns among the elderly." Still, not much is known about the effects of the long-term use of this hormone, so most researchers advice caution.

Much has also been made of the so-called "melatonin miracle." But rigorous testing of melatonin's effects on human beings has not been done yet. There is lot more on melatonin in Chapter 8.

So far, estrogen replacement therapy is the most effective hormone treatment. Epidemiological evidence suggests that supplemental estrogen after menopause helps prevent osteoporosis. But recent research has undercut claims that estrogen therapy reduces the risk of heart disease and dementia. Using estrogen does slightly increase the risk of ovarian cancer and promotes the growth of existing breast tumors. Estrogen may delay the onset of certain diseases that become more common as women grow older, but there is no evidence that it increases users' life spans.

Testosterone levels generally drop in men as they age. Research on testosterone has lagged behind estrogen research, perhaps because of the unsavory treatments of the past and perhaps because of steroid abuse among athletes. There are some indications that testosterone replacement can provide benefits to older men, including increasing muscle tone, overcoming erectile dysfunction, and improving their overall sense of well-being. On the other hand, it might promote the growth of any pre-existing prostate tumors. There are other unwelcome side effects, including increased hairiness and acne. And there is no evidence that testosterone supplementation will increase longevity.

The Genetic Imperative

Looking further down the road, once the genes that promote disease (Alzheimer's, diabetes, cardiovascular problems) and those that promote longevity are identified, it will become possible for parents to select favorable genes for their progeny. Already, more than 1,000 healthy children have been born after their parents used pre-implantation genetic diagnosis to select among eight-cell embryos to find the ones that were free of disease genes. In the future, parents might also select embryos that bear longevity-promoting genes and implant those. Further in the future, parents will be able to add genes that improve their progeny's immune systems, mental acuity, and athletic abilities by installing artificial chromosomes.

The Cambridge gerontologist Aubrey de Grey wants to genetically engineer mitochondrial genes into the nuclei of cells, where they would be better protected from the ravages of free radicals. He believes that once those genes are better protected they will not be so quickly mutated into the free radical death spiral. Once the vicious circle of mitochondrial mutations producing ever more free radicals is broken, longer life should result, he argues.

Even further in the future, another method to improve how human cells protect themselves from the ravages of free radicals might be possible. Some animals, such as birds, have more effective anti-oxidant protective mechanisms. Using them as a model, we might tweak our own genes. This could be the moral equivalent of replacing human anti-oxidant genes with similar but more effective genes from birds.

An even more visionary approach has been suggested by Robert Bradbury, whose startup Robiobotics is investigating the possibility of repairing whole genomes by using bacteria to ferry artificial chromosomes into human cells. The genetically engineered bacteria would infect billions of a patient's cells and deliver artificial chromosomes carrying a suite of hundreds of genes specifically aimed at repairing the damage done by free radicals. Some genes on the artificial chromosomes might be replacements for damaged genes; others would be designed to enhance cellular DNA repair. Skeptics point out that our immune systems would likely do in Robiobotics' designer bacteria, but Bradbury suggests that the problem might be dealt with by using a transitory immuno-suppressive therapy that would give the genetically engineered bacteria an opportunity to reach their desired cellular targets.

Nanomedical Insurance

But this focus on biological interventions may be wrongheaded. After all, some argue, we don't fly because we sprouted wings, so neither will we live longer because we've fiddled with our genomes. Why not make machines that hunt down harmful disease organisms and repair damaged cells? That is the ambitious aim of nanomedicine.

Nanotechnology is the science and technology of building devices using single atoms and molecules. A nanometer is a billionth of a meter, a length that is just over the diameter of many atoms. Conceptually, nanotechnology and biotechnology are not all that distinct. In the words of Rita Colwell, the director of the National Science Foundation, "Life is nanotechnology that works."

Proponents of medical nanotechnology -- such as Ralph Merkle, a former research scientist at Xerox's Palo Alto Research Center and now a fellow at the Texas nanotech company Zyvex -- outline an ambitious vision. "Nanotechnology will let us build fleets of computer-controlled molecular tools much smaller than a human cell and with the accuracy and precision of drug molecules," Merkle declared in the Winter 1999 issue of the *Anti-Aging Medical News*. He added, "These machines could remove obstructions in the circulatory system, kill cancer cells or take over the function of subcellular organelles." Robert Freitas, author of the 1999 book

Nanomedicine, foresees a day when oxygen-carrying red blood cells could be supplemented by artificial respirocytes made of carbon that would be 200 times more efficient.

If that isn't wild enough, Freitas recently unveiled a scheme that would replace your entire circulatory system with a sapphire vasculoid weighing two kilograms. No heart, no blood -- just a system of nanotech machines that would ferry oxygen, carbon dioxide, nutrients, and immune protective machines throughout your body, all encased in nearly unbreakable sapphire that would line your old-fashioned veins and arteries. Since 80 percent of what kills most people can be traced to the circulatory system -- heart attacks, strokes, wounding, metastasizing cancer -- such a vasculoid would dramatically increase one's life span. Freitas thinks the first models will be available in 40 years.

"With nanotechnology we could someday be rebuilding our own bodies, regenerating organs, slowing down aging," a bullish Samuel Stupp, professor of materials science and medicine at Northwestern University, predicted at a National Science Foundation conference earlier this year.

Pharmaceutical manufacturers are already building new drugs -- atom by atom, essentially -- to treat diseases. Merkle believes that it will be another 20 to 30 years before the visionary technologies he foresees will be available. In the medical arena, nanotechnology and biotechnology may well be destined to meld together.

Nanotechnology also plays a role in what some consider the second best alternative to living forever: cryonics. Cryonicists freeze people in liquid nitrogen with the idea that future technologies will be sufficiently advanced that the patients can be thawed out, revived, and cured of whatever ailments, including old age, afflicted them before they entered the deep freeze.

One problem facing cryonics enthusiasts is that no animal larger than a microscopic human embryo or a tiny tardigrade -- an insect that measures only a couple hundred microns across -- has yet been frozen and successfully revived. Freezing causes water in cells to expand, which disrupts them. But some researchers have developed a preservation technique called vitrification, essentially glassifying cells. This approach, it is claimed, causes far less disruption to cellular organization and destruction of cell walls. Scores of people have chosen to have either their full bodies or just their heads cryonically "suspended."

When it comes time to revive patients, the plan goes, nanotech machines will race through the patients' bodies, repairing the damage they have suffered from disease and freezing. Will it work? Who knows? Cryonicists put it this way: "The clinical trials are in progress. Come back in a century and we'll give you a reliable answer." Cryonicists divide the world into two groups, those who are experimenting with cryonics by being frozen vs. those who just die and are buried. Which would you rather be in, they ask: the control group or the experimental group?

The defining political conflict of the 21st century will be the battle over life and death. On one side stand the partisans of mortality, who counsel humanity to quietly accept our morbid fate and go gentle into that good night. On the other is the party of life, who rage against the dying of the light and yearn to extend the enjoyment of healthy life to as many as possible for as long as possible.

The most moderate critics of longevity simply worry that immortality would cause massive overpopulation. Worry not, says demographer Olshansky. If everyone on the planet were made immortal tomorrow, while maintaining the current projected trends in human fertility, world population would rise to around 13 billion by 2100. That, he notes, is the same number that alarmists like Paul Ehrlich used to predict for the middle of this century. Olshansky thinks that 100 years will give human society plenty of time to adjust to longer, healthier lives.

Death to Radical Mortalists!

Then there are the more radical mortalists, such as Fukuyama, Callahan, and Kass. Writing in the aforementioned issue of *First Things*, Leon Kass asserts that "to argue that human life would be better without death is, I submit, to argue that human life would be better being something other than human." Without the sound of time's winged chariot rushing at our backs, Kass claims, humanity would become frivolous, frittering away eternity with meaningless pastimes. Apparently, if we live longer, we'll just watch more *Baywatch* reruns and revisit Disney World.

For Kass, the sting of death makes for stronger friendships, greater loves, more ardent learning, and nobler deeds. But the fact of human mortality has also led people to commit all manner of villainy, cowardice, and crime. If one man nobly sacrifices his life to save his family and friends from invaders, it is because those invaders have themselves overcome their fear of death to seek glory, goods, and dominion. Gilgamesh wanted to avoid the oblivion of eternity, so he built a city, fought wars, and sought glory so that his name would ring down the ages.

Meanwhile, the names of all those thousands crushed under his tyranny -- those who labored to build the walls and temples of his city -- are lost for all time. The certainty of death may cause us to aspire, but not necessarily to the fulfillment offered by the gentler virtues.

Kass also points to the "undesired consequences of medical success in sustaining life, as more and more people are kept alive by artificial means in greatly debilitated and degraded conditions." Here he is engaged in what might be called Struldbruggism, after an episode in *Gulliver's Travels*. Gulliver visits the land of the Luggnuggians, among whom are occasionally born immortals called Struldbruggs. This is no blessing, since the immortals still grow older, weaker, and sicker.

But the goal of research on aging is not to turn us into a race of miserable Struldbruggs. As Olshansky puts it, "We don't want to make ourselves older longer, we want to make ourselves younger longer." Characteristically, Kass ignores the real goals of anti-aging research, misleading readers with a gruesome scenario in hopes of frightening them into embracing his pro-death dogma.

Future generations will look back at the beginning of the 21st century and marvel that intelligent people actually tried to stop biomedical progress just to protect their cramped and limited vision of human nature. But the chances that the Kassians will actually hold back longevity seem small. "It's too alluring," says Olshansky. "It's been the dream of humanity forever. How can we not?" Austad agrees. "People want this so badly, it's going to happen no matter what the government does," he predicts. "The government can help or it can hinder this research, but it will happen."

"A dramatic increase in lifespan is inevitable," Aubrey de Grey said in the British *Sunday Times* two years ago. "We understand aging at the molecular level sufficiently to not just imagine interventions to retard aging, but enough that we can describe them. It's an engineering project now, not a scientific one. We just don't know how long it will take." To which we can say: Hurry up! The 22nd century looks too interesting to miss.

Chapter 7

KEEPING YOUNG WITH BIOCHEMICALS

The "anti-aging" doctors promote hormone replacement, intravenously administered vitamins and a myriad of other therapies along with dietary changes and weight management as a way to stave off the effects of aging.

"We can kind of call anti-aging medicine 'inner plastic surgery' because it kind of works from the inside out. So if somebody is considering liposuction, I say, 'Please let me help you optimize your hormones. Maybe if you're over 40, even consider growth hormone, and let's see how good it can get for you in three months,' " says Dr. Donald Fisher, a former emergency medicine doctor who now runs an anti-aging medical practice in south Florida, the epicenter of the anti-aging medical movement.

Nationwide, the market for anti-aging medicine is estimated at more than $60 billion, with Florida the No. 1 state. According to the American Academy for Anti-Aging Medicine in Boca Raton, 9,852 of Florida's 58,896 doctors, 17%, have incorporated some element of anti-aging medicine into their practices. California, with 9,113 anti-aging doctors, is second. "Anywhere that vanity's important, you'll see a lot of this," says Dr. Mark Rosenberg, who opened an anti-aging practice in Delray Beach in 2003.

While the sector's growth is being fueled by affluent Baby Boomers eager to recapture their youth, the field is also attractive to physicians fed up with high caseloads and the hassles of dealing with insurance companies. Because insurers won't cover many anti-aging treatments, anti-aging physicians generally operate on a fee-for-service basis. They benefit in several ways: Treatments are lucrative, patients pay upfront in cash, and since the physicians don't need administrative staff to process insurance claims, they can hold down their office expenses.

Malpractice insurance rates are also considerably lower. Dr. Jennifer Landa, an OB/GYN who opened an anti-aging practice in Maitland three years ago, says her medical malpractice premiums ran about

$100,000 a year when she was delivering babies. As an anti-aging specialist, she pays less than $10,000 a year. Freed from the constraints of insurance reimbursement rates that dictate a high patient volume, Landa is able to devote considerably more time to her patients, most of whom come to her looking for relief from the symptoms of menopause and andropause or male menopause. While the average physician might spend about eight minutes with a patient, an initial visit with Landa lasts about an hour, and follow-ups generally last 30 minutes.

Anti-aging treatments typically involve some combination of a customized nutrition and fitness program along with hormone replacement therapy using "bioidentical" hormones, which are derived from plant oil and altered to become identical to human hormones such as estrogen and progesterone. Anti-aging doctors believe bioidentical hormone replacement therapy (BHRT) is safer than synthetic estrogens and progesterones that have been shown to increase a woman's risk for heart disease, stroke, blood clots and cancer.

Landa charges her female patients $495 for initial lab work that includes both blood and saliva testing. Men pay $595. Once the test results are in, an initial consult costs $495. Prescriptions for hormones like estrogen, progesterone and testosterone can average $35 or more each per month per hormone. Follow-up lab tests run about $250, and follow-up office visits are $275. Add in the costs of various "nutriceuticals" recommended by the doctor, and a typical patient taking two hormone supplements might spend upward of $3,000 annually.

With celebrities like Suzanne Somers singing the praises of BHRT, Landa and other anti-aging doctors say they've had no shortage of patients willing to pay big bucks to feel more like they did in their 20s or 30s.

Linda Gloria, a 57-year-old physician practice management consultant in Coral Springs, says she began seeing Dr. Fisher five years ago when she was in the throes of perimenopause, the period when a woman's body begins to transition into menopause. "After the birth of my last child at 43, I didn't feel quite right with the hormones. I had gone to my regular OB/GYN who said that after three kids, that's normal — but a week out of the month I wanted to kill everyone."

Fisher diagnosed Gloria with several hormone deficiencies and put her on a regimen of bioidentical progesterone, estrogen and testosterone. He also helped her fine-tune her diet and exercise routine. Gloria says the regimen has made a huge difference. Sleep comes easily now, she says, and she finds that she is calmer and able to tolerate everyday stresses better than before. Moreover, she has been able to avoid the hot flashes and other uncomfortable symptoms associated with menopause. Gloria is so pleased with the results that she encourages her friends who are in their 40s and 50s to get their hormone levels tested. "Just because you're in your 50s, doesn't mean you have to turn into an old lady."

Some testimonials for anti-aging medicine come from the doctors themselves. Every five months, Dr. Ferdinand Cabrera, a 49-year-old internist who runs the Genesis Health Institute, an anti-aging practice outside of Fort Lauderdale, has slow-release testosterone pellets implanted under his skin. He also takes a supplement to boost his production of HGH, and he takes 20 milligrams of melatonin each night to improve his sleep. A food sensitivity test revealed that his body was reacting to 34 foods, including almonds, watermelon, cantaloupe, eggplant, rice and wheat. He eliminated the offending agents from his diet. Like many anti-aging and holistic medical practitioners, Cabrera believes that low-level inflammation at a cellular level caused by foods we eat contributes to many chronic ailments, ranging from arthritis to type 2 diabetes and many autoimmune diseases.

Of course, Cabrera can't prove he's actually stalled or reversed his body's aging process, but he says he feels "fantastic" since he's made all the changes. His skin appears to have more elasticity, his thought processes are clearer, he's sleeping better and he's lost 20 pounds, he says.

Not everyone in the medical community is sold on the anti-aging practices, however. Views of the new field range from skepticism to warnings that anti-aging doctors are creating a threat to public health by casually prescribing substances like HGH. Dr. Thomas Perls, attending physician in the geriatrics section at Boston Medical

Center who has published a number of peer-reviewed articles on aging and anti-aging medicine, says HGH's side effects can range from tissue swelling and joint pain to enlargement of the heart and increased pressure around the brain. Some studies have also indicated that growth hormone enhances the ability of cancer to spread, he says.

"We have an anti-aging industry and other areas of the market that do an unbelievably good job of marketing an incredible false sense of safety and an incredible false sense of tremendous benefits from these drugs — and out of that comes a huge amount of money," Perls said in testimony before Congress last year. The National Institutes of Health offers a slightly less alarming view of the trend. The National Institute on Aging, a division of the NIH, urges consumers to "be skeptical of claims that hormone or other supplements can solve your age-related problems." Instead, consumers should focus on "what is known to help promote healthy aging: Healthy eating and physical activity." Moreover, the NIA advises against taking any supplement touted as an anti-aging remedy, arguing that there is "no proof of effectiveness, and the health risks of short and long-term use are unknown."

S. Jay Olshansky, a professor in the School of Public Health at the University of Illinois at Chicago and a research associate at the Center on Aging at the University of Chicago, points out that anti-aging medicine is not recognized by the American Medical Association as a medical specialty. That's important, he says, because there is, in fact, "no such thing as an anti-aging medicine. If there was an anti-aging medicine that was demonstrated to work, the whole world would be on it."

Olshansky acknowledges that some practices promoted by anti-aging doctors — eating less, eating healthier and exercising more — are good for everybody. "And that's a good thing," he says. But, he asks, "Are they reversing their aging? No. Are they influencing their aging in any way? No evidence for it."

The American Academy for Anti-Aging Medicine (A4M) and co-founders Robert Goldman and Ronald Klatz, meanwhile, have been sensitive to criticism. In 2005, A4M filed a $240-million defamation suit against Perls and Olshansky, alleging that the two professors had conspired to undermine the group's credibility and harmed the group's business prospects. Olshansky countersued, and both sides later dropped their lawsuits and reached a confidential settlement. In August, A4M sued Wikimedia Foundation and 10 anonymous Wikimedia contributors, alleging that an A4M Wikipedia page contained false and defamatory information about the group and its founders.

The internet, meanwhile, is awash with claims and promises by anti-aging clinics. "Turn Back the Hands of Time," the Naples Longevity Clinic proclaims on its website. "Rejuvenate your life ... be younger than your years through anti-aging medicine ... slow down the aging process."

Reached by phone, Dr. Lee Raymond Light, who runs the Naples Longevity Clinic, has a more modest description of the services he offers. "I'm not saying this is the fountain of youth. What I'm saying here is we're going to try to help you slow the natural aging process down to where God and nature intended it to be. "Today the maximum life span is 120 to 124 years," he says. "We're not saying we're going to get you there, but we can get you to live closer to that, with less disability, less joint problems, without the loss of libido."

The Anti-Aging Medicine Chest

Bioidentical Hormone Replacement Therapy (BHRT):
Bioidentical hormones are plant-derived hormones that are frequently prescribed to treat the symptoms of menopause and andropause, the decline of testosterone in men. The custom-mixed formulas are derived from yams or soybeans and then altered to be identical in molecular structure to those produced by the body. Many advocates of BHRT tout it as a safer, more natural alternative to conventional hormone replacement therapy. The U.S. Food and Drug Administration, however, says there is no evidence that bioidenticals are any safer or more effective than traditional FDA-approved menopausal hormone therapies.

Dehydroepiandrosterone (DHEA): This hormone is secreted by the adrenal glands and serves as a precursor to sex hormones such as estrogen and testosterone. Levels peak around age 25 and gradually decline with age. By the time a person is 70, DHEA levels are just 10% to 20% of what they were in the second decade of life. Promoters claim that restoring DHEA levels with supplements will increase muscle mass, bone growth and fat burning as well as improve memory and boost the immune system. A 2008 Mayo Clinic study concluded that there's no proof that DHEA has any anti-aging benefits.

Antioxidants: Many scientists suspect that free radicals — the unfettered oxygen particles that are produced during normal metabolic processes and by such activities as smoking — are a primary culprit behind aging. Common antioxidants recommended to help mop up these free radicals include vitamins A, C, and E and co-enzyme Q10. Polyphenols, which are found in red wine, fruits such as grapes, pomegranates and berries and tea and coffee, are also effective free radical scavengers.

Fish Oil: Omega-3 fish oil is a natural anti-inflammatory. Evidence from studies suggests it lowers triglycerides and reduces the risk of death, heart attack, dangerous abnormal heart rhythms and strokes in people with known cardiovascular disease. It also decreases blood pressure slightly.

Melatonin: This hormone is produced by the pineal gland, which is located beneath the brain, each night in response to darkness to help induce sleep. It is linked to the regulation of circadian hormonal rhythms, but levels may decrease as we age. Melatonin supplements are often prescribed to help patients sleep better.

Biochemicals that Occur Naturally in Our Food

Maintaining health and delaying aging involves different complex mechanisms. We can now control or partially control these mechanisms in our favor by the effective use of *biochemicals* (chemicals involved in the function of living organisms). These biochemicals are not powerful drugs, but occur naturally in our foods. Many of these are synthetically available as familiar nutrient supplements such as vitamins, minerals, amino acids, and nucleic acids. The proper availability of the biochemicals either from food or synthetic source is imperative for maintenance of efficient metabolism, which is necessary for providing energy and vitality.

However, the concentrated intake of these biochemicals can interfere with metabolic reactions. We know that excessive vitamins taken as supplements are either excreted from the body, stored in body fat and other organs, or used by the body as drugs to perform other, non-vitamin functions. It is the body buildup or storage of the excess that often causes serious side effects. Intelligent use of these chemicals, especially from natural food sources is the safe practice to follow.

We will concentrate here on biochemicals that can positively affect such activities as memory and depression, immunity, sleep problems, and sex drive. These chemicals can save from damaging mechanisms such as free radicals (as discussed in preceding chapters) that promote aging. These chemicals can also reduce serum cholesterol and thus help with high cholesterol related heart problems. Many of the chemicals have proven effective against killer diseases like cancer.

Moreover, the biochemicals described here can improve the vigor and vitality of those already in good health and can contribute to their overall efficiency, and go further to add productive years to their lives.

The foods that increase body level of certain biochemicals, can give sick people a new lease on life and save others from common diseases of heart and cancer.

Biochemicals and Their Effects on Various Body Systems

The human metabolism requires several biochemicals to keep various body systems in good working order. These biochemicals are generally supplied by various foods in different amounts. Sometimes foods in a diet are ideally balanced to supply the required biochemicals for maintaining and fostering efficient functioning of body systems. More often, however, these do not. Gaining knowledge about various foods, of course, is important to ensure supply of these chemicals. But the knowledge about specific biochemicals involved in specific body systems is important, so that synthetic forms of manufactured biochemicals can be utilized for increasing the efficiency of one's system. This section reviews briefly some of the biochemicals and their involvement in main body functions (Table 7.1).

Nervous Systems: Several amino derivatives (vitamin B-complex, some amino acids or alcohols) are required for building neurotransmitters, which regulate functioning of the nervous system. Shortage of neurotransmitters can cause all kind of problems, such as loss of memory, depression, and senility. Foods, such as liver, lecithin, milk, wheat germ, soybeans, and fish are rich in a vitamin like substance *choline,* which improves brain functioning. Choline sparks increase in *acetocholine* and thus brain function.

Table 7.1. Chemicals that affect our moods and performance

Activity (Function)	Name of Chemical	Source
Brain Function (Memory)	Choline (3 g/day) Vitamin C, B-12	Lecithin, milk, fish beef, soybeans, wheat germ
Depression (due to low level of neurotransmitters)	Vit. B-6, C Phenylalanine (100-500 mg/day)	Carbohydrate rich foods-Cookie, pasta
Immunity and blood circulation	Dimethyl glycine	Seeds
For pain relief and wound healing	Dimethylsulfoxide (DMSO)	Trees
For digestion improvement	Trimethylhydroxy glycine (Betaine)	Beets
For high serum Cholesterol	Niacin (vit. B-3) (3 g/day)	
Protection from free radicals	Vitamins C and E	
For higher alcohol consumption	Cysteine vitamin C	Eggs, orange juice
For Sex Drive	Protein	Milk, grains, sea-food

Immune System: Certain vitamins such as vitamin C (ascorbic acid), vitamin E (tocopherol), and vitamin A together with zinc and nucleic acids strengthen the immune system. A healthy immune system is required for destroying harmful germs and for removing defective blood cells and foreign substances from the body. White blood cells, which are manufactured in the spleen, kill disease causing bacteria.

Blood Vascular System: Nutrients such as lecithin with linoleate oil and vitamins C, B-6 (pyridoxine), B-3 (niacin), and E can help with atherosclerosis and arteriosclerosis--both associated with clotting of blood vessels. Polyunsaturated fatty acid called *omega-3* found in fish (sardines, salmon, trout, mackerel and even tuna) and monounsaturated olive oil (almonds and avocados also contain monounsaturated fat) can slow down the potentially clotting process by lowering cholesterol and triglycerides. Some vegetarian foods that lower cholesterol include onions, garlic, eggplant, avocado, and soluble-fiber-rich foods like oats. These degenerative diseases of the blood vascular system often appear with advancing age and cause gradual deterioration of the metabolism. During atherosclerosis, the formation of deposits in some of the arteries causes resistance to the bloodstream. These deposits may contain calcium, which hardens the arterial walls and diminishes their flexibility, thereby reducing one's capacity for strenuous activities.

Note: Aspirin stops existing blood platelets (which have eight-day lifespan) from clumping. One tablet (325 mg) every-other-day or baby aspirin (80 mg) every day is normally recommended to be effective on new platelets. By the way, aspirin not only lessens the risk of heart attacks and other diseases of the blood vascular system but also retards cataracts, quiets gum disease, increases immunity to infection, and of course, reduces headaches and other pains.

Digestive System: The special biochemicals called enzymes are required to breakdown the large macromolecules of protein, carbohydrates and the fats during digestion of food. Proper digestion of food for absorption into blood and lymph system is required for assimilation by the cells. Shortages of these hydrolytic enzymes can interfere with complete digestion and can cause stomach and intestinal disorders followed by premature aging. Betaine (methylated amino acid) hydrochloride can restore the supply of enzymes in the stomach and improve absorption of nutrients.

Arthritis and Skin: Biochemicals such as vitamin C, niacin (vitamin B-3), procaine (a diethylaminoethanol ester known as Gerovital), and dimethylsulfoxide (DMSO) can provide relief from arthritis. Vitamins A and E, and DMSO, and natural ingredients in herb *Aloe vera* can be used for skin disease.

Some Specific Biochemicals to Delay Aging and to Maintain Youthful Health

Having discussed effects of biochemicals on various body systems, we can now consider the numerous biochemicals recommended and used for prevention or delaying of aging.

Nucleic Acids: Nucleic acids prevail in two main groups: The ribonucleic acids (RNA) and Deoxyribonucleic acids (DNA). Nucleic acids are found in plants and animals and by digestion are hydrolyzed by enzyme action into purine, pyrimidine, pentose (sugar), and phosphate. These blocks are then recombined by enzymes in the body into one's personal nucleic acids.

The materials for nucleic acid formation and proteins are supplied by nutrition. Sugars and phosphates are nearly always available, but the bases, purines, and pyrimidines, are either synthesized from amino acids or isolated from hydrolyzed proteins. The enzymes needed for these catabolic and anabolic processes are supplied by the glandular system of the body. Usually this system is very effective in young metabolism but less so in aging systems. Therefore, a few biologists are recommending nucleic acids as supplements to nutrition.

Dr. Benjamin Frank, author of *No Aging Diet,* prescribes many foodstuffs rich in nucleic acids such as sardines, salmon, calves' liver, beets, beans, asparagus, onions, mushrooms, spinach, etc. to be consumed together with a high vitamin supplement and liberal amounts of milk, fruit juices, and water. Some of these foods do not contain the nucleic acids themselves but supply their precursors--the amino derivatives for synthesizing purines and pyrimidines needed for the nucleic acids. Asparagus, for example, contains asparagine, the amine of aspartic acid that is convertible into a pyrimidine derivative (see also chapter 4 for foods that supply nucleic acids).

Free Radicals Scavengers: The best free radical scavengers for potential human use include vitamin E, the element selenium, the food additive BHT (bis-hydroxytoluene), possibly vitamin C, and amino acids containing sulfur in the -SH form, specifically cysteine and methionine. All these inactivate *free radicals* (Free radicals are highly reactive chemical substances with an unpaired or missing electron whirling around a superactivated oxygen atom. For this reason they are highly reactive entities, which can damage membranes, DNA, and other parts of the tissues.) and theoretically could avert damage if delivered to the cellular sites that need protection.

Dr. Roy Walford of UCLA recommends the following list which he himself takes daily in divided doses:

Vitamin E 600 International Units

Selenium 160 micrograms

BHT 250 milligrams

Cysteine 300 milligrams

Methionine 120 milligrams

Ascorbyl palmitate 600 milligrams
(food preservative like BHT)

Vitamin C 1,000 milligrams

Bioflavinoids 300 milligrams

He recommends to take the first six just before or during meals and the last two after or between meals. The list includes substantial but perhaps not excessively large doses of the antioxidants. And one should keep in mind possible side effects and consult with their physician.

Besides antioxidants, a number of other substances which have given positive results in life-span studies include pantothenic acid (part of the B complex), several brain-reactive drugs such as DMAE, and possibly procaine or Gerovital. The following are the doses again Dr. Roy Walford of UCLA takes:

Calcium pantothenate 1 gram per day, in two doses
(vitamin B-5)

DMAE (Deaner) 120 milligrams per day, in one dose

There are still other suggestions that have been made to slow down aging. These include hormone preparations, lipofuscin inhibitors, lysome membrane stabilizers and cross-link inhibitors. However, the use of these substances, in the absence of conclusive data, is dangerous. Researchers are also testing compounds like DHEA that is shown to retard aging, fight fat, reduce blood cholesterol and prevent cancer. It is found in the human body in greater quantities than any other steroid hormone, and it declines precipitously with age. Scientific findings on many of these are already discussed in earlier chapters including the two mentioned below.

Human Growth Hormones (HGH)is produced as we sleep, the pituitary gland near the base of the brain secretes a protein consisting of 191 amino acids that flows into the bloodstream. Although the substance, Human Growth Hormone (HGH), remains in the bloodstream for only a few minutes, its impact on the body is dramatic. When HGH binds to receptors on target fat cells, it stimulates the breakdown of triglycerides and suppresses the cells' ability to store fat. At the same time, HGH triggers the liver to produce a potent anabolic hormone called IGF-1, a messenger molecule that stimulates bone, cartilage and muscle growth.

While levels of HGH peak during the rapid-growth phase of adolescence, they drop off as we age, at a rate of about 14% to 20% per decade. By the time we reach our 60s, our HGH level can be as little as 15% to 20% of what it was during our youth.

Most doctors consider declining levels of HGH and other key hormones, like testosterone, DHEA, melatonin, thyroid hormone, progesterone and estrogen, to be a normal part of aging. But a new crop of physicians says it doesn't have to be that way.

For quite some time, studies about the human growth hormone and the possibility of supplementing it when the body sans the capability to produce enough has been ongoing. The results of those studies have been favorable and so HGH supplements became known to man. Some brands went far ahead by adding up other ingredients that are supposed to help you feel and look youthful no matter what age you may be.

Again, they are not bad. They cannot be harmful if you know how to use them properly. If you think that continuing your destructive lifestyle is okay just because you take on anti-aging supplements, even if they increase HGH levels or have ingredients in them like Resveratrol, think again. Your body is for you to take care of. You can get some help from drug companies that manufacture health and anti-aging supplements but you need to move to a healthy lifestyle yourself. That is, if you want to take advantage of the quality of life that populations like Abkhazians enjoy past the 100 mark.

Melatonin, is a hormone of 1990s, which is produced by the pineal gland as darkness falls. Researchers have claimed extraordinary benefits that melatonin can offer:

• **Age reversing:** Melatonin can extend our lives by decades while keeping our bodies "young."

• **Disease fighting:** Melatonin can help prevent heart disease, cancer, and other common diseases.

• **Stress relieving:** Melatonin can protect us from the destructive effects of chronic stress.

• **Cycle restoring:** Melatonin is a safe, non-addictive sleeping agent that can cure disruptions in our sleep/wake cycle, such as jet lag and insomnia.

The next chapter is devoted to this miraculous substance and it's link to aging, and the right doses of melatonin that should be tried.

Chapter 8

THE MELATONIN WAY TO YOUTH

Melatonin is a natural hormone that resets the body's clock. It's secreted in the dark by the pineal gland, a pea-size structure at the center of the brain, as our eyes register the fall of darkness. Studies suggest that low-dose supplements can not only hasten sleep and ease jet lag, but researchers believe that melatonin could help counter the ravages of age.

In test-tube and animal experiments, researchers have found that Melatonin protects cells from free radical damage, strengthens the immune system and slows the growth of some cancers. Of course, there are surer routes to good health as discussed earlier in the guide -- old standbys like exercising, eating right, controlling stress, and giving up bad habits such as smoking. But to lot of Americans, the lure of a safe, cheap, "natural" panacea is proving irresistible. People are going crazy for this so called natural stuff. The health food stores could hardly keep it on the shelf. And the melatonin craze has been almost as good for publishers as it has been for health-food stores.

Melatonin **BENEFITS** are still debatable, but studies point to many possible uses.

Jet Lag: Studies have shown the melatonin can help reset your body's clock after jet lag. About 50 percent of people in studies were able to reset their body's internal clock faster using low-dose melatonin supplements for a few days.

Delayed Sleep Phase Syndrome: This is a condition in which a person sleeps a normal amount, but their sleep is delayed into late in the night (not because of TV or other reason). Research shows melatonin is promising for treating this syndrome.

Insomnia in the Elderly: Research is promising that melatonin supplementation can help treat insomnia in older adults. Studies show trends that look good, but the studies were not well-designed and left many questions unanswered. Most studies only looked at short-term effects (a few days). But melatonin does seem to ease insomnia.

Sleep Problems in Children with Neuro-Psychiatric Disorders: There is also some promising research that melatonin could help children with conditions such as autism, psychiatric disorders or epilepsy improve their sleep. This use of melatonin is being investigated.

Sleep Improvement for Healthy People: There is also good evidence that melatonin helps improve sleep in healthy people. The studies shown that melatonin, taken by mouth about 30 to 60 minutes before sleep, will shorten the time it takes to fall asleep. More research is needed to determine the long-term effects of melatonin supplementation.

Other Uses (unclear evidence):

- improve sleep in people with Alzheimer's disease

- used as an antioxidant to protect cells from free-radical damage.

- used to treat ADHD (attention deficit hyperactivity disorder) and ADHD-related sleep problems

- help to taper benzodiapepines (used for insomnia, anxiety, seizures, and muscle spasms).

- for bipolar disorder-related sleep problems

- in treating cancer or preventing cancer (not enough research to know about interference with other treatments and overall effect)

- treatment of chemotherapy side effects

- regulate circadian rhythms in blind persons

- for depression-related sleep disturbances

- to treat glaucoma

- to prevent headaches

- Prevent pregnancy (in large doses)

- Boost the immune system

- Lower blood cholesterol and prevent heart disease

- Extend Life

- and many, many other conditions.

The **complaints** so far are very few, and primarily were not life-threatening such as headache, disturbed sleep with few reports of nightmares, daytime drowsiness, gynecomastia (breast enlargement in men), and depression. However, certain classes of people should probably **AVOID** Melatonin. The people who should avoid include pregnant women, people with severe allergies or autoimmune diseases, healthy children (who already produce it in abundance), and women who are trying to get pregnant (since high doses can act as a contraceptive). People who have a history of depression, in particular, should discuss the use of melatonin with their doctors before taking it.

In this chapter, we will describe melatonin and it's link to aging, and the right doses that should be tried.

MELATONIN PRODUCTION AND THE PINEAL GLAND

Melatonin is ubiquitous in nature, cells, plants, animals, tissues and any living organism. Milk, vegetables, cereals, rice, meat, etc., contain variable amounts of melatonin.

Melatonin is produced from serotonin with the help of several associated enzymes and co-factors, while serotonin is produced from the amino acid tryptophan, which is found in a wide variety of high-protein foods such as meat, fish, milk, and cheese. Melatonin is also found in small amounts in bananas, tomatoes, and other fruits and vegetables.

Melatonin also is produced in smaller amounts in the gastrointestinal (GI) tract and other parts of the body. The pineal gland contains the highest central nervous system concentration of serotonin in the body, and produces the largest amounts of melatonin as well as other neuroendocrine hormones.

Every day, as darkness sets in, melatonin production (from serotonin) in the pineal gland is rhythmically induced via cyclic AMP activation of beta receptors by the neurotransmitter norepinephrine through the action of the enzyme N-Acetyltransferase (NAT), which results in low levels of serotonin and high levels of melatonin, with a peak level occurring about 2 AM. During daylight hours, on the other hand, light entering the pineal gland through the eyes, blocks NAT's induction of melatonin, which results in high levels of serotonin and low levels of melatonin.

The Serotonin/Melatonin Ratio: The pineal gland has weak regenerative abilities because its primary cells (pinealocytes) are of neuronal derivation. The number of pinealocytes in the pineal gland is genetically predetermined, and these non-dividing cells are not replaced when they are lost due to biological or chemical injury.

"As we grow older, our pineal gland atrophies, eventually reaching a state of organ failure, as cells are constantly lost for a variety of reasons. The decline of the pineal is accelerated by the accumulation of calcium deposits, which cause the organ to harden and interferes with its activities.

According to Dr. Rozencwaig, the age related decline of the pineal gland means that there are fewer and fewer pinealocytes available to produce melatonin from serotonin, which leads to lower levels of melatonin and higher levels of serotonin, and that the resulting change in the serotonin/melatonin ratio is responsible for much of the deterioration experienced throughout the body with advancing age.

He points to evidence that increasing levels of circulating serotonin may be responsible for the increased incidence of certain types of cancer, and that high levels of serotonin are associated with platelet adhesiveness leading to atherosclerosis, the primary causes of heart attacks and strokes.

He also points to Dr. Segall's tryptophan-deprivation experiments, which, he believes, lowered only extra pineal serotonin levels, leading to a major decrease in the incidence of cancer and other degenerative diseases, as well as extended life span and reproductive capacity in laboratory rats.

The Regenerative Ability of Melatonin: In 1987, when Rozencwaig, at al. published their hypothesis about the role of melatonin in aging, there was relatively little evidence to support it. Yet the extent to which they anticipated future research advances is remarkable.

It was pointed out, for example, that night is the time of replenishment, when our bodies recuperate by regenerating our tissues and restoring our glycogen reserves. Since melatonin is the natural agent that prepares us for sleep and circulates in peak amounts while we sleep, it almost certainly plays a major role in the regenerative process. The fact that melatonin is extremely effective at penetrating the blood-brain barrier indicates that it may be especially beneficial in the repair, regeneration, and rejuvenation of the brain during sleep. Among the anti-aging effects of melatonin mentioned by Dr. Rozencwaig in the 1987 paper is the fact that melatonin stimulates natural antioxidant levels, improves DNA repair mechanisms, and enhances our neuroendocrine and immune systems.

In a subsequent update in Pscyhoneurocndocrinology (Vol. 18, No. 4, pgs. 283-295, 1993) Grad and Rozencwaig discuss the evidence in support of their hypothesis. Among the effects of melatonin discussed in this paper is its ability to block pregnancy, boost immune function, improve the quality of sleep, regulate the endocrine system, protect against cancer, stimulate natural antioxidants, and protect against cardiovascular disease by inhibiting platelet aggregation and ischemia.

"The Melatonin Deficiency Syndrome is perhaps the basic mechanism through which aging changes can be explained in terms of a single causative lesion, a lesion that causes the progressive patterns of change seen in the older population. In addition, pineal rhythmicity is the only biological clock synchronized with a time dimension, which also has the capacity to repair and rejuvenate the organism. Since the pineal gland's action to delay development is known, it is not surprising that it would also act to delay developmental senescent changes and extend the life span. In addition, it raises the possibility of the reversal of senescence....This may require replacement of melatonin along with other hormones in order to achieve a more youthful endocrine balance and homeostasis, and consequently a possible repair of the body as a whole."

Dr. Rozencwaig who is from Montreal, Canada also uses a serotonin antagonist called Periactin (Cyproheptadine) to treat the diseases of aging. He says that the results he gets with Periactin are similar to those he gets with melatonin and that he, sometimes, uses both agents together. We are not aware of any independent studies to verify various claims about treating his patients about aging, cancer and other diseases with melatonin and similar therapies.

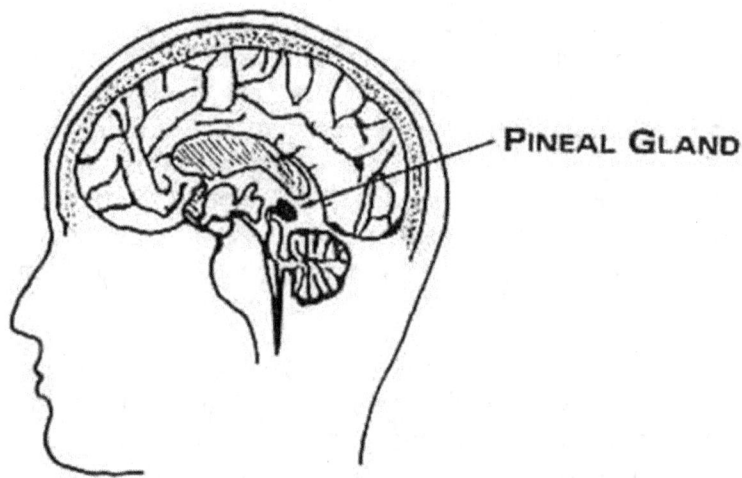

PINEAL GLAND

Fig 8.1. The Pineal Gland which produces melatonin

The role of pineal gland, however, is verified by several independent studies. It now appears that the pineal gland is, in fact, the biological clock that controls aging, and that this gland's daily production of melatonin establishes the basic rhythm of life for every organ, every tissue, and every cell within the body. Melatonin also regulates other biological rhythms--the cycle of sleep and wakefulness and the onset of puberty, for example. Melatonin has been shown to protect us from many of the physical changes we associate with aging--everything from heart disease and menopause to memory loss and insomnia. It's secreted cyclically from the pineal gland, a pea-sized structure located at the center of the brain, melatonin keeps us in sync with the rhythms.

Melatonin production is regulated, in large part, by the daily cycle of lightness and darkness:

1. As darkness falls, the pineal gland produces a surge of melatonin that goes to all parts of the body.

2. When light hits the retina, neural impulses signal the pineal gland to slow melatonin production.

NOTE: The melatonin production in the gut is not affected by light and dark. However, melatonin production increases in the digestive tract when calories are restricted. This may explain why dietary restriction can increase the life span.

Common agents which antagonize synthesis and secretion of melatonin: Alcohol, corticosteroids, beta-blockers (especially in the evening), caffeine, nicotine and many chemical substances with pharmacological activity can antagonize the synthesis and secretion of Melatonin. But melatonin does not itself antagonize the activity of any drug.

CHANGES IN MELATONIN PRODUCTION WITH AGE

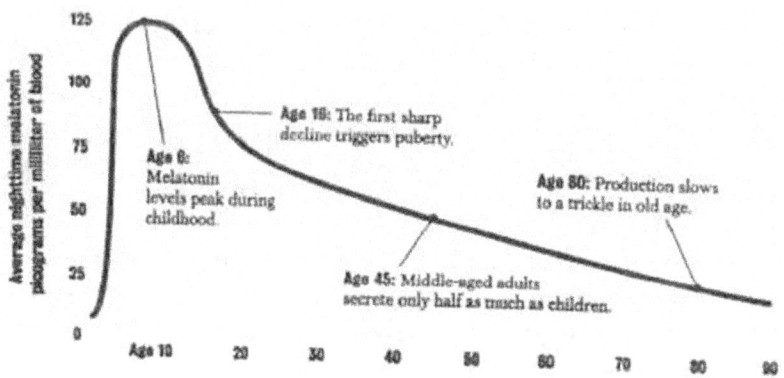

Fig 8.2. Changes in Night Time Melatonin Production with Age

It appears that melatonin levels peak in childhood and then decline with age. Why is this? Scientists are not sure, but they have some

---

hypotheses. Initially it was thought that calcium slowly depositing in the pineal gland was the culprit. As the gland was calcified, less melatonin was secreted at night. However, the more accepted hypothesis holds that the cells within the pineal gland decrease in number as we age, making it less efficient in producing melatonin.

Here're the age-related changes in melatonin production throughout the life:

• Melatonin levels peak during childhood at age 6 producing about 125 picogram per milliliter of blood.

• At Age 16, the production shows sharp drop to about 70% when it triggers puberty.

• At middle age of 45, the production is about half (50%) as much as in children.

• At an old age of 80, the production is less than one-fourth as much as in children.

HOW DOES MELATONIN LINK TO AGING?

In 1991, an Italian Researcher, Pierpaofi and a Russian scientist, Vladimir Lesnikov, reported a dramatic experiment that gave direct and incontrovertible proof of the **pineal gland's** control of the **aging process.** They bred two groups of mice that were genetically identical in every respect, and raised them under identical conditions. There was only one difference between the groups: The first group was young-three to four months of age; the second group, at an age of about eighteen months, was well into retirement age in mouse years.

The researchers swapped the old and young pineal glands in a microsurgical brain operation. All 10 of the "old" mice now had youthful pineals, while the 10 young mice had aged glands.

At first, not much happened. Because all the mice were genetically identical, their bodies accepted the new organs without any complications. Then, as the weeks passed, the young mice began to fail, showing unmistakable signs of accelerated aging. The older mice were rejuvenated. By the end of the experiment, there was little doubt about the pineal gland's role in aging: The young mice with the "old" pineals lived an average of only seventeen months--about two-thirds of the normal life span. The old mice who had received the "young" pineal glands, by contrast, lived for thirty-four months -- twice as long as the first group, and almost half again longer than the normal life span!

The conclusion: If the pineal does not age, we cannot possibly age, or at least the aging process will never again be as we have seen and experienced it until now.

Melatonin, Restricted Calorie Diet, and Aging

A restricted caloric diet (RCD) is the first historical approach to significantly retard aging, so the question is: **Has melatonin a relation to a low calorie diet?** In other words, does a low calorie diet modify melatonin and conversely does melatonin mimic a restricted caloric diet? Is there a common denominator which will affect the inherited longevity program of each individual?

All the findings prove that a diminished calorie intake will significantly delay aging and the many aging related diseases and their metabolic dysfunctions. However, it took more than sixty years before the *National Institute on Aging* started to evaluate whether or not a RCD (Restricted Calorie Diet) applied to non-human primates would also retard aging. There is now evidence that this is the case and many results begin to be available from this long-term trial.

It is believed that a *different* hormonal regulation could be responsible for the aging-postponing effects of a RCD. In other words, the aging-postponing effects of a RCD produce permanent changes in the central, hypothalamic-pituitary hormonal functions, thus maintaining the body at a more juvenile level of endocrine and metabolic regulation. This was particularly clear with regard to sexual functions of rodents maintained at a RCD.

Scientific studies demonstrate that if mice are kept at a RCD for a few weeks after weaning, and then fed again *ad libitum*, they maintain (in spite of this normal feeding) a permanently different pattern of hormonal regulation. This data confirmed that the feeding behavior (at a time when the neuroendocrine system is still immature), permanently affects maturation and function of the entire neuroendocrine system. This observation is of course very relevant with regard to the onset of obesity in overfed children and the consequent permanent derangement of their mature neuroendocrine and metabolic system and irreversible obesity. This *environmentally induced obesity* (which is now so dramatically evident in the affluent Western Society) is of course different from mild or severe fattening of "normal" metabolic aging in humans. Also, this environmentally acquired dietary obesity is different from *genetically inherited obesity,* which however afflicts a small number of families and individuals. The clear answers from many studies all indicate that a RCD produces juvenility-oriented and permanent changes of neuroendocrine regulation.

If endocrine and metabolic dysfunction are the expression of the program of aging, and if the pineal gland is a "life and aging clock", consequently we must consider that a RCD affects mainly the pineal gland and its functional state. This seems to be the case. It has been reported that a RCD maintains juvenile levels of melatonin in rodents.

In a collaborative project with Dr. George Roth and Mark Lane at the National Institute on Aging, Baltimore, USA, in which large groups of primates have been under a RCD for several years, **data is emerging that RCD very significantly maintains high levels of nocturnal melatonin in both male and female aging monkeys, comparable to the levels in young primates**. The conclusion is that a RCD, by setting the "neuroendocrine clock" at a more juvenile level, protects the pineal gland from aging and thus protects from aging the whole pineal-controlled hormonal, circadian and seasonal periodicity, whose progressive decay leads to aging.

From studies on the pineal gland, which secretes the hormone melatonin, researchers have learned that aging isn't something that afflicts our hearts, our kidneys, our skin, our eyes, or our minds. The changes that occur in these and other organs are the outward symptoms of a process that begins at the hormonal level.

And aging isn't something that just happens to us when we're old. It starts even before we're born. At different stages of life, we call it by different names. In infants and small children, we call it childhood development, and it's generally viewed as a positive process: As children's bodies mature, they acquire important abilities and skills. In later years, we call the process puberty and then adolescence, as the body undergoes physical and mental changes. Then come two or three decades in which the body becomes less efficient. We may put on weight, lose our hair; our skin becomes less elastic and more prone to damage; and we can't reach those long fly balls anymore. Health problems begin to come up more frequently. Even so, the physical changes between the ages of, say, nineteen and forty-five occur far more gradually than those that come before and after.

As we move toward our sixth and seventh decades, change comes more quickly once again. In women, menopause produces profound physical alterations that go beyond the question of fertility. In men and women alike, significant and potentially fatal health effects begin to occur: heart disease, hypertension, high cholesterol, increased risks of cancer, changes in brain function, and others. For different people, the pace is different but the patterns are similar; ultimately one or some combination of these degenerative diseases leads to death.

How We Age

At each of these stages of life, the pineal gland undergoes corresponding changes. In the first three months of life, the pineal gland secretes little or no melatonin. Once melatonin production begins, however, it really picks up steam. As children, our melatonin levels are at the highest they'll ever be in our lives (see Fig 8.2 in this chapter showing melatonin changes with age).

The changes of puberty are now believed to be triggered by declining melatonin levels in the blood. Interestingly, though, melatonin production remains fairly steady up to and through puberty. What changes is body size: As we grow larger, the concentration of melatonin in the bloodstream becomes less; in effect, the same amount of melatonin must now serve a larger body. (This finding has lead to the speculation on the link between obesity and such disorders as heart disease. As the body gets bigger, the concentration of melatonin may become diluted, giving rise to these degenerative diseases)

After adolescence, however, the pineal gland gradually begins to reduce the amount of melatonin that it produces for a number of reasons: Like other parts of the brain, the pineal gland doesn't replace lost cells; once they're gone, they're gone forever. Also, calcium deposits build up within the pineal gland over time. It's not clear what effect this calcification has, but it seems to interfere with the gland's ability to function efficiently. One group of researchers speculates that the accumulation of calcium deposits in the pineal gland gradually diminishes the function of the pineal gland. In old age, this degeneration reaches the point that the pineal gland produces virtually no melatonin whatsoever.

A Conclusion and Melatonin Theory of Aging

This research on the parallel progression of aging and decrease in melatonin levels, along with the laboratory experiments, now gives us a revolutionary new view of the aging process. It isn't just a collection of unrelated problems that overtake us as the years go by. It's a carefully orchestrated process that begins in the pineal gland. And most significant of all, it's a process that can be controlled.

We can formulate many practical implications of this new view of aging, and at the ways in which we can put melatonin to work for us today. But first, consider the profound shift in scientific thinking that this new view represents.

Of course, we have not reached the point that we entirely understand the mysteries of aging--and we probably never will. But now we have a new way of looking at the problems of aging--a view that gives us insights into how many of the seemingly unrelated aspects of aging may in fact be interrelated at the most fundamental levels of biology. Melatonin research is giving us, for the first time, a new view of aging. Aging is seen less and less in metaphysical terms--as a process that is largely beyond the reach of science--and more and more in chemical and physiological terms, as a process that can be influenced by scientific intervention, as a treatable condition.

These new discoveries will not, of course, close down the heart centers, nursing homes, or oncology clinics, but may push the diseases they treat off to later years and help prevent many cases of cancer, heart failure, and other diseases of aging. Nor will an increase in melatonin replace the need for exercise, a low-fat diet, and other elements of a healthy lifestyle that we have discussed in earlier chapters, but, it may add to their benefits. In short, this theory of aging gives us new ways of looking at one of mankind's oldest mysteries and practical strategies that we can begin to follow now.

TAKING RIGHT DOSES OF MELATONIN

Melatonin works in tandem with the pineal gland, the body's regulator, to monitor and govern our other body systems--and offers benefits varying from age reversing, disease fighting, stress relieving to cycle restoring. When the pineal gland falters, whether the failure is due to a disruption in circadian cycles from jet lag, or the breakdown in pineal function due to aging, melatonin will help to boost our regulator back to its peak capacity. If the pineal gland is working well, so does the rest of the body. When the pineal gland is out of whack, it throws our other body systems off balance.

Without a doubt, the best melatonin is the homegrown variety--that is, the melatonin manufactured in our own body. But no matter how well the clock runs, eventually it runs down. Inevitably, as we grow older, our natural wellsprings of melatonin begin to dry up. The declining melatonin levels can, however, be overcome with oral supplements.

So **when and how much melatonin do we need** to take in order to get our body back in sync? The question of when we should take melatonin and how much to take will depend on the problem that we are seeking to correct. The regimen for age-reversal is markedly different, for example, from curing jet lag or insomnia. In this section we will break down the guidelines for dosage information and instructions for taking melatonin according to each of the specific problem areas that melatonin addresses. (Although our main emphasis is on slowing the aging process, a brief reference is made to other important problems that melatonin is found to correct.)

But first, let us set some general guidelines and common sense precautions. The recommendations are based on studies of how melatonin naturally works within our bodies. While some literature may recommend much larger doses than suggested here, it is generally believed that, to gain the optimal benefits of melatonin, more is not necessarily better. We are aiming to approximate the balance of hormone levels that naturally occurs when we are youthful and in our peak health. To artificially boost our melatonin level above that youthful level is not in keeping with our natural approach.

Bearing in mind that while the principle that overarches all of our thinking is to restore melatonin to our youthful level, we do not need melatonin supplementation for children. The reason is simple. In childhood melatonin production is already at its highest level and therefore it need not and should not, except in very special circumstances, be boosted higher.

It's important to suggest against melatonin supplementation to women during pregnancy and lactation. The reason for this is again very simple. In pregnancy, the mother is already naturally transmitting melatonin to the fetus via the placenta, and to increase the mother's melatonin level would in turn increase the amount delivered to the fetus, which is something that should be avoided.

DETERMINING THE MELATONIN DOSES FOR AGE REVERSAL

Our melatonin replacement strategy is to restore our melatonin level to what it was when we were in our twenties. After that, the level drops off very gradually, until we reach our mid-forties, when a dramatic decline in our melatonin production occurs. This decline steepens with each passing year, so that by the time we are eighty, our melatonin level is way down what it was when we were in our twenties (see Fig 8.2). Our strategy therefore is to reverse this downward curve and maintain our melatonin level at its constant, youthful peak. Doing this is not complicated. All that is necessary is to take the amount of melatonin required to bring our level up to its youthful baseline. That means we only need to take a small dose in our forties, a slightly larger dose in our fifties, more in our sixties, and so on. By restoring our melatonin to its youthful level we restore the function of our body's aging clock--the pineal gland--and help maintain our body in the youthful state. (see dosage Table 8.1)

We know from research that in most people, the level of melatonin begins its most precipitous adult decline at about age forty-five, so this is a good time to begin our melatonin replacement therapy. However, not all of us fit into this norm. Depending on our genes, this falloff may begin earlier or even later. If you have a family history of what we call the diseases of aging, such as cancer, cardiovascular disease, and heart disease, beginning melatonin replacement as early as your thirties or early forties may help you overcome a genetic predisposition to these problems.

Although it is unnecessary for younger adults to begin an age-reversing program with melatonin, and is not recommended below the ages specified, it is fine for adults of any age to use melatonin to cure other problems. If you are an adult of any age, including a young adult, who wants to treat jet lag or a sleep disorder such as insomnia, for example, you may take melatonin on a short-term basis to resolve those specific problems. (See dosage instructions for jet lag and sleep disorders at the end of this chapter.)

Most experts don't believe that by starting replacement therapy earlier than forty you can get a head start on reversing the aging process. Nor should those of you who are in your fifties or older think that if you haven't already started taking melatonin by the time you were forty five that you have missed the boat. On the contrary, by restoring melatonin levels to their youthful peaks you can produce age-reversing benefits no matter when you begin.

Table 8.1. Melatonin doses you need.

Age	Dose of Melatonin	Time to Take
40-44	Take .5 to 1 mg	at bedtime
45-54	Take 1 to 2 mg	at bedtime
55-64	Take 2 to 2.5 mg	at bedtime
65-74	Take 2.5 to 5 mg	at bedtime
75 Plus	Take 3.5 to 5 mg	at bedtime

Melatonin Doses You Need: To maintain your melatonin levels at their youthful peaks, the following dosages are recommended at various ages. These dosages are based on normative levels of melatonin in adults as they age and the amount of supplement required to restore levels to their youthful peaks.

You will notice that it is consistently recommended that melatonin be taken at bed time and that the dosage increases with age. For most people, melatonin induces drowsiness and it is best to take it just before sleeping. If you find that the recommended dosage leaves you groggy in the morning, that means the dosage is too high for you and we recommend that you reduce it by approximately .5 mg at a time until you find the right level for you.

When you go to your health-food store or pharmacy, you will find that melatonin comes in capsules and tablets, typically in strengths of 2, 2.5, and 3 mg. If the right dosage for you is lower, simply do the following:

For tablets: Break a tablet to the size that you need. For example, if you have a 2 mg tablet and you want a 1 mg dose, break the tablet in half. If you want to take a .5 mg dose, break the tablet into quarters.

For capsules: if you have a 3 mg capsule and want to take a 1 mg dose, empty the contents of the 3 mg capsule into a small dish. For the first dose, mix approximately one third of the contents with an ounce of liquid. (Store the remaining contents in a small, covered dish in the refrigerator.) For the second dose, mix approximately one half of the remaining melatonin with an ounce of liquid. For the third dose, mix the remaining melatonin with an ounce of liquid.

The time to take melatonin is very important. Melatonin should only be taken at night, before bed. Remember, as darkness falls, it tells our pineal gland to release melatonin, which in turn tells our body that it's time to sleep. Therefore, it's not surprising that most people will find that melatonin makes them somewhat sleepy. The typical recommendation to take melatonin is about **half an hour before bedtime;** some nutritionists recommend the dose an hour or two before bedtime. Try the timing that works for you. If you are a nightshift worker, your daytime bedtime, rather than the usual night time, governs when you take your dosage. After taking melatonin, don't engage in activities that require a state of alertness, such as driving or operating machinery. Although melatonin will not make you feel "drugged" in the way that a narcotic sleeping pill does, you may feel relaxed and drowsy and ready for sleep.

Which Brand to Buy: There are a variety of companies producing melatonin, and it is readily available in most health-food stores and many pharmacies. Different brands offer different doses in their capsules or tablets. There are two forms of melatonin available: (1) the synthetic forms, and (2) the so called natural melatonin, made from the extract of animal pineal glands. We prefer and recommend synthetic melatonin. . In addition to being less expensive, synthetic melatonin allows greater quality control: It's free of impurities and the potency is standardized. Synthetic melatonin is, generally, extracted from beans and is white in its pure form. But, a good indicator of product purity is color, darker preparations may have other ingredients contained within them. Your pharmacist can help you select the correct product.

Melatonin for Sleep and Jet Lag: it is important to mention the melatonin doses for sleep and jet leg, although this guide is primarily devoted to aging. If you are already taking melatonin daily as a part of age-reversal therapy, it is all right to follow the instructions below for sleep and jet lag. However, do not exceed a total of 5 mg daily.

For Sleep: Start with 1 mg and increase your dose by 1 mg every twenty minutes until you reach a maximum of 5 mg. (Remember, not to exceed a total of 5 mg daily.) Once you have determined the right dosage that work for you--stick with it. By continuing with melatonin for two weeks, you should have reset your body clock. When you stop taking melatonin after two weeks, you should continue to sleep even without melatonin.

For Jet Lag: If you are taking a trip that involves travel across time zones, take 3 to 5 mg of melatonin prior to bedtime once you reach your new destination. Continue to take melatonin at bedtime for four nights or so until your body clock is completely reset. When you return home, readjust your body clock by taking 3 to 5 mg of melatonin before bedtime, and do so for 4 nights or less until you have readjusted to the time change.

How about melatonin for disease prevention, especially heart disease and cancers We suggest you talk to your physician, even though melatonin has been called an age-reversing, disease-fighting, and sex-enhancing hormone.

Summary of Scientific findings about Melatonin

Melatonin was discovered in 1958 and named for its skin-bleaching effect upon melanin (skin pigment).

Melatonin is N-Acetyl-5-Methoxytryptamine, which is a mammalian hormone synthesized from serotonin, mainly in the pineal gland, but some is also synthesized in the retina, bone marrow and lymphocytes. The pineal gland and the retina synthesize melatonin in the absence of light, that is, at night or in darkness. Light does not inhibit melatonin synthesis in other tissues. Green light (505 nanometers) is the most effective for suppressing melatonin production [THE JOURNAL OF CLINICAL ENDOCRINOLOGY & METABOLISM; Brainard,GC; 86(11):433-436 (2001)].

Melatonin is not only a natural mammalian hormone, it is widely found in nature, including foods such as oats (1.8 nanogram melatonin per gram of oats).

Melatonin for Sleep: Melatonin is a natural sleep-inducing agent. Because daylight reduces melatonin production, blood levels of melatonin are usually high at night and low during the day. Artificial light reduces melatonin production. Shift-workers who sleep in darkened rooms with their eyes closed can increase melatonin production during daylight hours. For people who sleep "normal hours", natural melatonin production peaks between 2 am and 4 am, with the peaks becoming smaller with advancing age after early childhood.

Melatonin given as supplements during daytime causes feelings of sleepiness and fatigue, which can adversely affect performance [PROCEEDINGS OF THE NATIONAL ACADEMY OF SCIENCES (USA); Dollins,AB; 91(5):1824-1828 (1994)]. The fact that melatonin production declines so drastically with age probably explains many of the sleep disturbances seen in the elderly. Low doses of melatonin (0.3 mg) given as a supplement seem to be as effective for inducing sleep as higher doses. But because the plasma half-life of melatonin is less than an hour, time-release supplements of higher doses are more effective for sustaining sleep. Unlike sleep induced by benzodiazepine drugs, melatonin-induced sleep does not suppress Rapid Eye Movement (REM) sleep and slow-wave sleep-- and does not result in "hangover" feelings the next day [CLINICAL PHARMACOLOGY AND THERAPEUTICS; Zhdanova,IV; 57(5):552-558 (1995)]. Nonsteroidal anti-inflammatory drugs such as aspirin (which disturbs sleep), decrease plasma melatonin levels [PHYSIOLOGY & BEHAVIOR; Murphy,PJ; 55(6):1063-1066 (1994)].

Melatonin and Aging: Melatonin plasma levels in mammals decline considerably with aging after early childhood, which might be a factor in the greater vulnerability of elderly people to infections. People over age 60 may show no increase in melatonin production at night. Lifespan studies on mice and rats have shown significant lifespan increase as a result of melatonin supplementation, when given to older rodents and when co-administered with Thyrotropin-Releasing Hormone (TRH is also produced in the pineal gland) [JOURNAL OF ANTI-AGING MEDICINE; Pierpaoli,W; 2(4):343-348 (1999)]. Typically, only supplements given at nighttime are effective.

In children, nocturnal melatonin production decreases significantly at puberty. The decrease is more strongly associated with the stage of puberty than with chronological age [THE JOURNAL OF CLINICAL ENDOCRINOLOGY & METABOLISM; Salti,R; 85(6):2137-2144 (2000)].

Antioxidant Actions: (For background on free radicals and antioxidants, see earlier Chapter 2 on Aging Theories) Melatonin is a very powerful anti-oxidant. Unlike Vitamin C or glutathione, which are only active in aqueous (watery) phase and Vitamin E, which is only active in lipid (oily) phase, melatonin is effective in both aqueous and lipid phases. Unlike Vitamin E and Vitamin C, which cannot readily cross the blood-brain barrier, melatonin easily crosses the blood-brain barrier [EXPERIMENTAL BIOLOGY AND MEDICINE; Reiter, RJ; 230:104-117 (2005)]. **(If you don't understand any of the scientific findings, just ignore them. The bottom line is melatonin protects from the damage caused by**

free radicals and antioxidant which are one of the causes that we age.)

Melatonin is twice as effective at protecting cell membranes from lipid peroxidation as Vitamin E [PHARMACOLOGY LETTERS; Pieri,C; 55(15):271-276 (1994)]. Melatonin is five times more effective than glutathione for neutralizing hydroxyl radicals -- the free radicals normally responsible for more than half of all free radical damage in the body (causing lipid peroxidation, DNA damage and protein oxidation). Melatonin and adenosine may be particularly important in protecting brain cells because glutathione concentrations are not very high in the brain. Melatonin in combination with deprenyl significantly counteracts hydroxyl radical production associated with dopamine autoxidation in the brain, and the combination effect is significantly greater than the effect of either agent alone [JOURNAL OF PINEAL RESEARCH; Khaldy,H; 29(2):100-107 (2000)].

In one study, melatonin was more than 60 times more effective than Vitamin C or Vitamin E in protecting DNA from DNA damage [ENVIRONMENTAL HEALTH PERSPECTIVES; Qi, W; 108:399-402 (2000)]. Melatonin may bind to DNA, providing further protection beyond anti-oxidant activity.

Melatonin concentrations are particularly high in mitochondria and the cell nucleus. DNA in mitochondria are particularly vulnerable to damage because mitochondria have fewer DNA-repair enzymes than nuclear DNA and because mitochondrial DNA lack the protective histone proteins which nuclear DNA have. By its ability to penetrate readily into mitochondria, by directly protecting mitochondrial DNA and by inducing antioxidant enzymes in mitochondria, melatonin may greatly protect mitochondria. Melatonin demonstrably protects mitochondrial DNA from the damaging effects of ethyl alcohol binges in brain, heart and skeletal muscle, as well as in the liver [JOURNAL OF PHARMACOLOGY AND EXPERIMENTAL THERAPEUTICS; Mansouri,A; 298(2):737-743 (2001)]. Twenty-five years after proposing the free-radical theory of aging, Denham Harman proposed a mitochondrial free-radical theory of aging based on the observation that mitochondria are the source of most cellular free radicals [PROCEEDINGS OF THE NATIONAL ACADEMY OF SCIENCES (USA); Harman,D; 78(11):7124-7128 (1981)]. Fruit flies given melatonin increased maximum lifespan by one-third and median lifespan by one-eighth [EXPERIMENTAL GERONTOLOGY; Bonilla,E; 37:629-638 (2002)]. Along with its antioxidant actions, melatonin directly facilitates mitochondrial electron transport chain enzymes in the production of ATP (energy rich molecule produced in mitochondria during respiration/ breathing) [THE INTERNATIONAL JOURNAL OF BIOCHEMISTRY & CELL BIOLOGY; Martin,M; 34(4):348-357 (2002)].

In addition to the hydroxyl and peroxyl radical, melatonin neutralizes superoxide, singlet oxygen, hydrogen peroxide and hypochlorous acid [ANNALS OF THE NEW YORK ACADEMY OF SCIENCES 959:238-250 (2002)]. Melatonin inhibits peroxynitrite formation by inhibition of the enzyme nitric oxide synthetase in some brain tissues [LIFE SCIENCES; Leon, J.; 75:765-790 (2004)]. Melatonin increases gene expression and activity of the anti-oxidant enzymes glutathione peroxidase, superoxide dismutase and catalase [JOURNAL OF PINEAL RESEARCH; Kotler,M; 24(2):83-89 (1998)]. The effect of glutathione peroxidase induction is considerable -- a four-fold increase of the antioxidant enzyme in brain mitochondria and an eightfold increase in liver mitochondria with a 100 nano-molar melatonin concentration [THE FASEB JOURNAL; Martin,M; 14(12):1677-1679 (2000)].

The chief metabolite of melatonin, 6-hydroxymelatonin (formed in the liver) has as much anti-oxidant activity as melatonin. In fact, the reaction products of melatonin with hydroxyl radical and hydrogen peroxide are themselves anti-oxidants [ACTA BIOCHEMICA POLONICA; Reiter,RJ; 54(1):1-9 (2007)]. Vitamin C can become a toxic pro-oxidant when exposed to free iron, and most anti-oxidants become weak free radicals after having neutralized a free radical. But melatonin's antioxidant action involves donation of *two* electrons, not one electron, thereby ensuring that melatonin does not become a free radical.

Ischemia/Reperfusion: Ischemia which means local anemia, can be described as an inadequate flow of blood to a part of the body, caused by constriction or blockage of the blood vessels supplying it.

Anti-oxidants are typically very useful against ischemia-reperfusion injury and melatonin is no exception. Melatonin has been shown to reduce cardiac arrythmias and to reduce oxidized lipids in the ischemic heart. Melatonin also reduces superoxide production and myeloperoxide (an enzyme in neutrophils which produces hypochlorous acid) during ischemia-reperfusion [CARDIOVASCULAR RESEARCH; Reiter, RJ; 58:10-19 (2003)]. Pretreatment of rats with melaonin 30 minutes before ischemia significantly reduced nitric oxide production, but 5mg/kg was twice as effective as either 1.5mg/kg or 50mg/kg [JOURNAL OF PINEAL RESEARCH;Pei,Z; 34:110-118 (2003)]. A similar experiment of ischemia-reperfusion in fetal rat brain mitochondria demonstrated a significant reduction in lipid peroxidation products [JOURNAL OF PINEAL RESEARCH; Wakatsuki,A; 31(2):167-172 (2001)]. Melatonin readily crosses the blood-brain barrier, and can protect neurons from excitotoxicity [EXPERIMENTAL BIOLOGY AND MEDICINE; Reiter, RJ; 230:104-117 (2005)].

Melatonin can also protect against ischemia-reperfusion injury by inhibiting inducible nitric oxide production, at least partially by means of inhibiting activation of the pro-inflammatory transcription factor NF-κB and blockage of NF-κB binding to DNA [THE FASEB JOURNAL; Gilad,E; 12(9):685-693 (1998)]. Nitric oxide has been shown to exacerbate apoptosis due to calcium release from the mitochondrial pool and activation of the Mitochondrial Permeability Transition Pore (**MPTP**) [THE FASEB JOURNAL; Horn,TFW; 16(12):1611-1622 (2002)].

Hormonal Effects: Alteration of the amount of daylight from season-to-season affects melatonin secretion, and thereby can affect seasonal fertility in many mammals. In deer, the decreased light during the Fall season leads to increased fertility and breeding. For hamsters, increased melatonin during Fall and Winter leads to testicular regression in males and estrus inhibition in females. Melatonin can suppress libido by inhibiting secretion of luteinizing hormone (LH) and follicle stimulating hormone (FSH) from the anterior pituitary gland. Humans may be similar to hamsters because pituitary-gonadal function and conception rates are lower for people living in the Arctic during Winter months [THE NEW ENGLAND JOURNAL OF MEDICINE; Brzezinski,A; 336(3):186-195 (1997)]. Melatonin can inhibit ovulation in women and has even been suggested for use in conjunction with other contraceptives [THE JOURNAL OF CLINICAL ENDOCRINOLOGY & METABOLISM; Voordouw,BCG; 74(1):108-117 (1992)]. A small study of men, however, showed no suppression of reproductive hormones with melatonin [HUMAN REPRODUCTION; Luboshitzky,R; 15(1):60-65 (2000)].

Melatonin interacts with the hypothalamic-pituitary-adrenal hormonal system to reduce the harmful effects of excessive glucocorticoids -- notably damage to the hippocampus [NEUROENDOCRINOLOGY; Konakchieva,R; 67:171-180 (1998)]. Melatonin is necessary for normal sexual maturation. Melatonin supplementation improves thyroid function and can delay the onset of menopause [ANNALS OF THE NEW YORK ACADEMY OF SCIENCES; Lopez,BP; 1057:337-364 (2005) and Bellipanni,F; 1057:393-402 (2005)].

Immune System Effects: Immune system cells are typically very vulnerable to free radical damage, which is why anti-oxidants such as melatonin are generally very effective in boosting the immune system. Melatonin may also reduce the age-related decline in thymus gland function [PROCEEDINGS OF THE NATIONAL ACADEMY OF SCIENCES (USA); Pierpaoli,W; 91(2):787-791 1994)].

Melatonin is of benefit for both cellular and humoral immunity. Melatonin stimulates production of the cytokines **InterLeukin−2 (IL−2)**, **InterLeukin−6 (IL−6)**, and **InterLeukin−12 (IL−12)**. Melatonin stiumulates the production of progenitor cells for granulocytes, macrophages, natural killer (**NK**) cells and certain helper T−cells (**CD4+**), while lowering harmful **CD8+** cell concentrations [IMMUNITY & AGEING; Srinivasan,V; 2:17 (2005)]. The combination of low T−cell proliferation and low CD4/CD8 ratio was highly predictive of low 2−year survival in a study of people in the 86−92 age range [JOURNALS OF GERONTOLOGY 50A(6):B378-B382 (1995)].

Melatonin and Cancer: Melatonin reduces estradiol levels in the blood and inhibits aromatase expression in human breast cancer cells, both of which suggest that melatonin could be of value in the prevention and treatment of breast cancer [JOURNAL OF PINEAL RESEARCH; Sanchez-Barcelo,EJ; 38(4):217-222 (2005)]. Because melatonin protects against the side effects of radiation, it could be a useful adjunct to radiotherapy in cancer treatment [JOURNAL OF RADIATION RESEARCH; Shirazi,A; 48(4):263-272 (2007)].

The most worrisome experiments involving melatonin are those that show increasing incidence of cancer in certain species of mice (usually female mice) that are given melatonin. Ironically, a study of this kind showed an overall 5.4% increase in mean lifespan and a 17% increase in maximum lifespan despite the increased incidence of tumors [JOURNALS OF GERONTOLOGY; Anisimov,VN; 56A:B311-B323 (2001)]. By contrast, melatonin in other strains of female mice has been shown to suppress tumors. The anti-cancer effects of melatonin are also seen in rats [BREAST CANCER RESEARCH; Lenoir,V; 7(4):R470-R476 (2005)].

Studies of human cancer cells show that treatment with melatonin reduces their proliferation and metastatic capacity [ENDOCRINE-RELATED CANCER; Sanchez-Barcelo,EJ; 10(2):153-159 (2003) and JOURNAL OF PINEAL RESEARCH; Cos,S; 32(2):90-96 (2002)]. Melatonin has been shown to directly inhibit breast cancer cells by 75% -- optimally at normal youthful body levels rather than higher doses [JOURNAL OF NEURAL TRANSMISSION; Blask, DE; 21:433-449 (1986)]. Melatonin is not mutagenic according to the Ames Test and, in fact, has been shown to reduce the mutagenicity of a number of chemicals [MUTATION RESEARCH; Musatov,SA; 417(2-3):75-84 (1998)].

A study of totally blind women (who would have less exposure to light and more exposure to melatonin) found them to have less than two-thirds the normal risk of breast cancer [BRITISH JOURNAL OF CANCER; Kliukiene,J; 84(3):397-399 (2001)]. Similar epidemiological studies on people with varying levels of light exposure provide further confirmation of the hypothesis that melatonin reduced cancer risk in humans. Other epidemiological studies have found no correlation between cancer and blood melatonin levels.

Alzheimer's Disease: With aging there is a decline in both serotonin transporters [LIFE SCIENCES; Yamamoto,M; 71(7):751-757 (2002)] and serotonin receptors [NEUROPSYCHO-

PHARMACOLOGY; Meltzer,MD; 71(7):751-757 (2002)].
Serotonin is the precursor for melatonin in the brain.

Although it remains unproven, there is evidence that free radicals may cause or aggravate Alzheimer's Disease. Elderly Alzheimer's Disease patients have half the blood levels of melatonin as normal people the same age. The amyloid-beta protein which is the most commonly implicated marker of Alzheimer's is most neurotoxic and most resistant to proteolytic degradation when it aggregates into beta-sheets. Melatonin inhibits the aggregation of amyloid-beta into beta-sheets [JOURNAL OF BIOLOGICAL CHEMISTRY; Pappolla,M; 273(13):7185-7188 (1998) and BIOCHEMISTRY; Poeggeler,B; 40(49):14995-15001 (2001)]. Melatonin also reduces the hyperphosphorylation of tau protein, which leads to the neurofibrillary tangles of Alzheimer's Disease [ACTA PHARMACOLOGICA SINICA; Wang,J;27(1):41-49 (2006) and CURRENT NEUROPHARMACOLOGY; Oritz,GG; 6(3):203-214 (2008)].

Possible Negative Effects: For melatonin, more is not better. Blood concentrations which are ten times normal youthful levels can cleave heme molecules to liberate iron and induce oxidative stress [NEUROCHEMISTRY; Clapp-Lilly,KL; 12(6):1277-1280 (2001)]. Even higher levels of melatonin concentrations deplete reduced glutathione levels [LIFE SCIENCES; Osseni,RA; 502:127-131 (2001)].

Melatonin can counteract the effectiveness of steroid drugs, can worsen allergic responses and can worsen auto-immune disease. Melatonin readily crosses the placenta, but the effects of above-normal quantities on a developing fetus or a pregnant woman have not been thoroughly studied. Melatonin is freely available in the United States and has been safely used by large numbers of people, so there are few financial incentives for large controlled clinical trials. Adolescents should not take melatonin supplements because melatonin can interfere with the growth and development that occurs after puberty. Consultation with a physician may be advised before taking melatonin supplements.

Dosing: Although supplement doses a hundred times the typical 3 mg per day have proven to be safe, higher doses may be unnecessary or even harmful. Doses in the 1 mg to 5 mg range should be safe and sufficient insofar as these doses produce blood levels 10 to 100 times higher than the usual nighttime peaks [THE NEW ENGLAND JOURNAL OF MEDICINE; Brzezinski,A; 336(3):186-195 (1997)].

Night-time blood levels of melatonin peak at about 120 picograms per milliliter just before the age of puberty. By age 30 blood levels have fallen by half and by age 60 the levels of melatonin in the blood are usually about 5 picograms per milliliter or less. Melatonin supplementation is of much more value for older adults, because their natural production of melatonin is so low [EXPERIMENTAL GERONTOLOGY; Pandi-Perumal,SR; 40(12):911-925 (2005)].

Because melatonin can cause drowsiness and is not very effective when taken in daylight, one or two time-release capsules or tablets daily at bedtime is preferable. Dosages in excess of
3 to 6 mg (milligrams) should not be necessary, and often lower doses are preferred, and equally effective for induction of sleep (if not the other benefits).

The summary of scientific finding is primarily for those who are interested in further research and information about melatonin.

Chapter 9

FUTURE OF AGING RESEARCH AND CONCLUDING REMARKS

A variety of techniques extend the lives of model organisms, and similar approaches might help human beings stay healthy longer

First let us look at what is known about aging from biological perspective, then we will conclude with possibility of genetic engineering to tinkle with age-related genes. Future role of nanotechnology in keeping us young and healthy is already discussed in chapter 6.

Aging: A Biological Perspective

People spend more time trying to avoid aging than trying to understand it. We deny aging at first and then—seeing its reality in the mirror—grudgingly accept it. In the past two decades, biological investigations of aging grew into cutting-edge science. Unfortunately, little of that intellectual excitement reaches the larger society.

As we learn more about aging, we will think more deeply about the consequences of our increasing ability to alter this biological process. To provide an overview of this field, this chapter defines aging in modern biological terms, describes our current understanding of the biological mechanisms that underlie aging, reviews successful cases of longevity intervention in laboratory animals and discusses the implications for humans. Taken together, this information makes an intriguing tale.

Living Longer: As early as 1840, life expectancy started increasing in Sweden. Soon, the trend appeared in other developed countries, too. In the United States, for example, white females in 1900 lived an average of 48 years; by 2000, they lived an average of 87 years. This 39-year increase in average lifespan really took hold by mid-century, largely due to reduced mortality before puberty, which killed 24 percent of the women born in 1900.

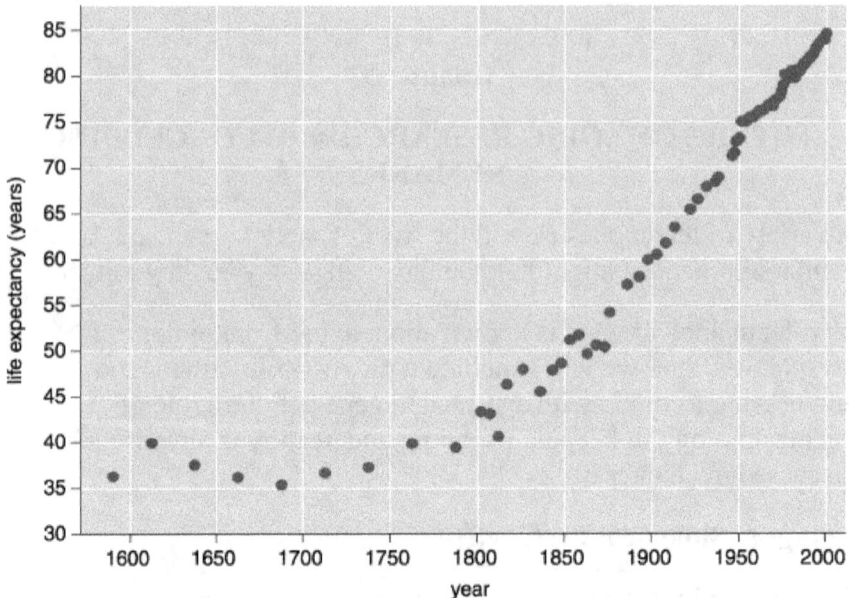

Figure 9.1. People live longer today than ever before. From roughly 1600 until 1800, the average life expectancy at birth oscillated between 35 and 40 years. After 1800, the life-expectancy curve started climbing, as shown here. By the year 2000, the average person could expect to live roughly 80 years. In many cases, these longer lives resulted from improved public health, including sanitary sewers and clean drinking water.

Young girls—no longer taken by accidents or infectious diseases— survived to die as old ladies. In the 1920s, extensive public-health measures, including sanitary sewers and clean drinking water, triggered this decreased mortality. Later, antibiotics and improved medical care increased average life spans even more. As the 20th century rolled by, the elderly grew healthier and mentally independent than their parents at the same ages. In addition, the average person lived longer than ever. Consequently, the probability of some proportion of them surviving for more than a century increased, as well.

Although social and medical interventions helped people live longer, none of the techniques affected the aging process. A healthy 65-year-old in 1900 would be physically indistinguishable from his or her counterpart in 2000. There are simply more 65-year-olds today because the past century's efforts reduced early mortality. If you do not die young, then you can live to be old, but you will still age as humans have throughout history.

Aging involves multiple deleterious biological events that accumulate in different tissues over time and gradually reduce an organism's state of maintenance and function. Calendar time, however, serves as an imperfect measurement of the physiological processes involved in aging. We all know individuals who are the same chronological age but appear to be very different physiological ages. Rather than counting years—or gray hairs, for that matter—modern gerontologists turn to biological markers, or biomarkers, of aging. These physiological parameters indicate an individual's functional level, and some biomarkers, such as insulin levels, correlate with mortality. The presence of such biomarkers depends indirectly on patterns of gene expression, which are induced by a variety of internal or external stimuli. If gene expression remains stable, so does an adult's overall health. In fact, extraordinary stability in gene expression can create a centenarian, but especially unstable expression can trigger premature mortality. If aging is a series of increasingly different molecular and physiological signatures, then senescence comprises the processes that are responsible for the changes in those signatures.

Is Aging Adaptive: "Nothing in biology makes sense except in the light of evolution," according to the well-known geneticist Theodosius Dobzhansky, and his statement applies to aging. By natural selection, some genetic variants of any population will be more successful—putting more copies of their genes into the next generation—than others, and the more numerous variants will be favored. Moreover, the high mortality rates resulting from predation, illness and accidents that are common among wild populations indicate that few, if any, individuals live long enough to show signs of aging and senescence. So any wild population consists primarily of young, breeding adults who make the genetic contributions to the next generation. Consequently, deleterious genetic variants that act late in life are not selected against because their carriers probably either die from environmental hazards before they reach old age or survive as post-reproductive adults. In either case, those genes are invisible to natural selection. In addition, long-lived genetic variants will not be selected for because they are expressed only in those few surviving post-reproductive individuals.

From an evolutionary perspective, the entire reproductive game revolves around passing copies of genes to the next generation. No trait, including extended longevity, provides evolutionary value unless it makes an individual more successful in this game. Living long enough to reproduce does merit evolutionary value, but living long enough to be post-reproductive supplies no increased fitness, at least in the case of non-social animals.

People already live long. Why then are we not capable of reproducing and living indefinitely or at least much longer than we do now? The answer involves energy. An organism must divide its energy between maintenance, repair and reproduction. Even a well-fed organism copes with energy limitations. As a result, organisms face a tough problem: What is the best allocation of finite metabolic energy to maximize reproduction and repair?

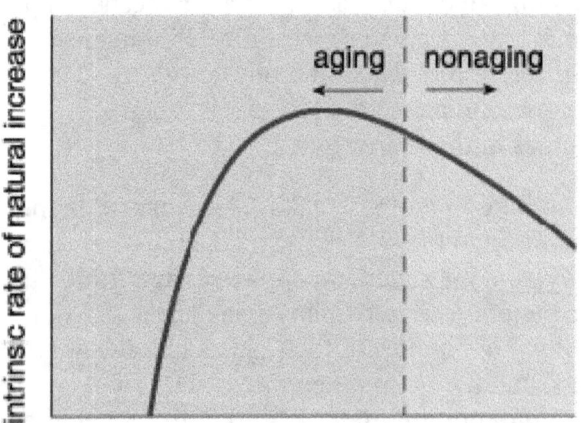

Figure 9.2. Energy allocation controls aging. An organism must divide its energy between maintenance, repair and reproduction. Thomas Kirkwood, when at the University of Newcastle Upon Tyne, showed that, in theory, as an organism puts more energy into repair and maintenance of body structure, including the gonads, *(x-axis)* it reproduces *(y-axis)* more at first. With even more energy applied to

maintenance, an organism's reproduction peaks and starts to decrease. Unfortunately for longevity, reproductive fitness peaks before an organism puts enough energy into repair to offset aging. In other words, reproduction requires less energy than does life-extending repair. As a result, an organism ages when energy allocations fail to make adequate repairs, not because of a genetically based aging program.

In 1977, Thomas Kirkwood of the University of Newcastle Upon Tyne showed theoretically that increasing the amount of energy expended on somatic repair results in increased survivorship but decreased fecundity, and vice versa. A choice must be made. Reproduction requires less energy than does repair. Therefore, allocating sufficient energy to maximize somatic repair will reduce fecundity, which decreases an organism's Darwinian fitness. In contrast, increasing fecundity will decrease the energy available for repair and probably result in a shortened longevity. In most cases, decreased fecundity over a longer life span yields fewer copies of an individual's genes in the next generation than does higher fecundity over a shorter lifetime. Accordingly, maximum fitness takes place at a repair level lower than that required for indefinite somatic repair, and organisms eventually die. This is the so-called disposable soma theory.

This theory reveals an intriguing point: **An organism ages when energy allocations fail to make adequate repairs, not because of a genetically based aging program.** As a result, humans are not required to age. So if people age only because there is no biological reason not to, then some intervention might stop—or at least slow—aging.

A Healthier Span: The lives of animals can be lengthened in three ways: increasing their early survival rate, increasing their late survival rate or delaying senescence. The first two approaches decrease the mortality rate at the beginning or end of life, respectively, but do not affect the basic aging process. Even with increased early or late survival, organisms age normally but seem to be somewhat more resistant to stresses that kill off their normal comrades. Humans who exercise, for example, survive at higher rates in early and middle life and experience a lower level of morbidity, or occurrence of disease, but they age normally, with no decrease in late-life mortality. Centenarians, on the other hand, live longer than most people, although no one would mistake a centenarian for a middle-aged person. Instead, centenarians age normally, but tend to be healthier than their ordinary fellows. Although athletes and centenarians provide interesting examples of increasing early and late survival rates, they shed little light on basic aging processes.

The most interesting alteration involves the third approach, delaying the onset of senescence. Many examples of this pattern exist in laboratory animals, but none in humans as yet. Robert Arking and his colleagues at Wayne State University, for instance, created long-lived strains of fruit flies through artificial selection—simply allowing only the longer-lived flies to breed with one another over several generations. When they compared ordinary and long-lived fruit flies, the average life was about 40 and 70 days, respectively. Likewise, the maximum lifespan increased from about 61 to 91 days. But how much of that added time is lived in good health? Let's call that good-health period the health span and make it the time from birth until ten percent of the initial population dies. For ordinary flies, the health span lasted 30 days, and it grew to 60 days in the long-lived flies. So the flies' health span doubled. Nonetheless, the senescent period—from the end of the health span until all of the flies died—remained the same, about 30 days, which is a smaller proportion of the maximum life span for the long-lived flies.

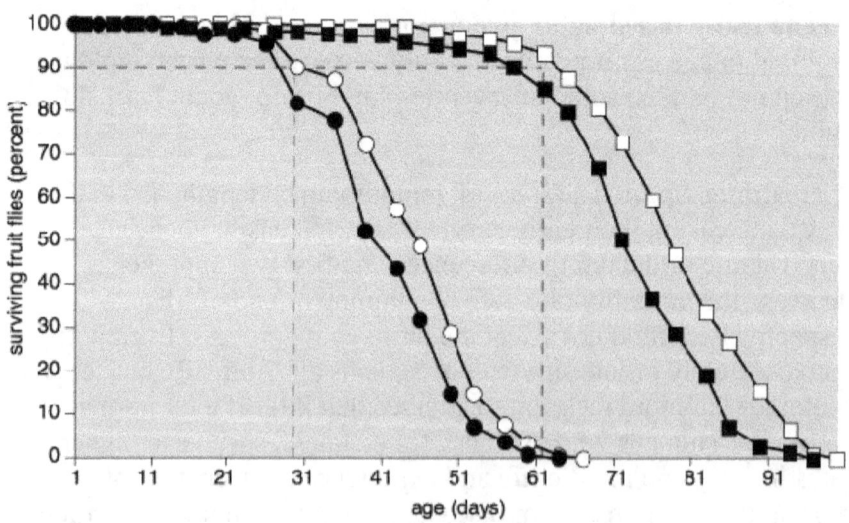

Figure 9.3. Breeding can extend the lives of fruit flies. Robert Arking and his colleagues created long-lived strains of fruit flies *(squares)* through artificial selection by simply allowing only the longer-lived flies to breed with one another over several generations. The normal-lived fruit flies *(circles)* lived an average of about 40 days and the long-lived ones lived about 70 days. The process is reproducible, as shown by the similar results obtained with two independent replicates *(black and white symbols)*. The author calls the "health span" the time from birth until ten 10 percent of the initial population dies, which is about 30 days *(first block on left marked with dotted lines)* for the ordinary flies and 60 days *(second block)* for the long-lived flies. These data reveal that increasing the health span can extend longevity without extending the "senescent span."

The data on fruit flies demonstrate that the health span and the senescent span are separate phases of the life span. Moreover, these data reveal that increasing the health span can extend longevity. In fact, experiments from a wide variety of investigators show that delaying senescence can increase longevity in all of aging research's model organisms: common brewer's yeast (*Saccharomyces cerevisae*), nematode worms (*Caenorhabditis elegans*), fruit flies (*Drosophila melanogaster*) and laboratory mice (*Mus musculus*). For example, Martin Holzenberger and his colleagues at the Institut National de la Santé et de la Recherche Médicale in Paris inactivated the insulin-like growth factor type 1 receptor (IGF-1R) in mice, and the health span of females, (but not males,) increased by about 75 percent. Such findings suggest a built-in potential for increasing the health span, and this potential has been exploited experimentally as described earlier and below.

Cutting Back the Calories: In 1934, Clive McCay and Mary Crowell of Cornell delayed the onset of senescence in rats by reducing how much they ate. In fact, reducing the calories in an animal's diet by about 40 percent, while keeping the different nutrients at normal levels, results in healthy and long-lived mice and rats. It also works for flies and worms. In fact, hundreds of studies show that caloric restriction lengthens life. Similar experiments are underway in macaque monkeys, and, although these long-term experiments are still in progress, the available data suggest that caloric restriction may lengthen primate lives, too. There is good evidence, put forth by Mark Lane and his colleagues at the National Institute on Aging, suggesting that caloric restriction utilizes a hormonal mechanism to exert its effects on all the different tissues of the body.

Caloric restriction creates measurable changes in a variety of biomarkers. For example, George Roth and his colleagues at the National Institute on Aging put male rhesus monkeys on a 30-percent reduction in calories for three to five years. When compared with control monkeys, the ones on reduced calories displayed significantly lower body temperature, reduced plasma levels of insulin and increased serum levels of dehydroepiandrosterone sulfate, a steroid hormone precursor molecule that commonly decreases in aging monkeys and humans. We do not yet known if these monkeys will in fact live long, but it is interesting to note that these same three traits were found in long-lived human males.

Scientists can also correlate gene-expression patterns with differential mortality for adults of different ages or who received different treatments. They can distinguish between gene-expression patterns of healthy and sick animals or young and old ones. They can even differentiate between normal-lived and long-lived animals. Several independent experiments indicate that each tissue has its own characteristic aging pattern. Skeletal muscle and heart muscle, for example, are very similar to each other, but they age in very different manners. Although both of these are different than neural tissue, certain broad functional similarities exist. All tissues show an increased stress response, likely coupled to increased levels of highly reactive molecules called reactive oxygen species (ROS), or less accurately free radicals, and to an increased level of cellular damage. Aging tissues also seem less capable of processing signal proteins or synthesizing and degrading other proteins. Both of these processes—increased ROS production and decreased signal sensitivity/protein turnover—might set off positive feedback cycles that progressively degrade an aging cell's performance in these and other areas.

Caloric restriction, on the other hand, brings about a variety of changes that seem to have the effect of maintaining the optimal function of the tissue by reducing the stress levels within the cell while retaining the optimal metabolic, biosynthetic and turnover capabilities of the cells. As a result, the **animals shift their focus from growth and reproduction to somatic repair and maintenance.** The **restricted animals** age more slowly and maintain their tissue integrity well into old age. They also show either a significant delay or a complete elimination of the onset of many age-related pathologies, and their survival curves are characterized by a significant extension of the health span. In addition to aging more slowly, calorically restricted animals stay physically healthier and mentally active much longer then normally fed controls. On the other hand, calorically restricted animals grow more slowly than normal, are often less fecund and are sometimes less resistant to environmental stresses.

Although reducing calories makes lab animals live longer, it hardly promises a reasonable approach for humans. Even if promised extended longevity, few people would willingly cut back on calories by 40 percent.

Cloning for Longevity: If calorie restriction isn't your cup of tea, regenerative medicine is the next best bet for near-term success. The most promising path to regenerative medicine is the controversial process known as therapeutic cloning. If you need a new heart or liver, it might be possible to grow a new perfect transplant using your own cells. The process would involve transferring the nucleus of one of your skin cells to an enucleated human egg, which would then grow in a petri dish to the blastocyst stage. Stem cells would be harvested from the blastocyst and transformed into the desired tissues for transplant.

Stem cells have been found in adult tissues, in umbilical cord blood from newborns, and in embryos. All have shown some promise. William Haseltine, the CEO of Human Genome Sciences, recently predicted in *The Washington Post* that it will one day be possible to "reseed the body with our own cells that are made more potent and younger, so we can repopulate the body." But stem cell transplants are at least 10 years away -- or even longer, if Leon Kass and his allies succeed in banning therapeutic cloning. Since the chorus calling for a ban includes President Bush, the prospects for research in this area are not as bright as they ought to be; even though President Obama is in favor.

Another problem: Regenerative medicine does not stop or slow aging. It just fixes the problems and diseases that accompany aging. In a sense, it's just a better form of conventional medicine. Continually trading in your old, worn-out organs for new ones is certainly better than the alternative, but it would be ever so much more pleasant if you could just stay young forever.

Unsweetened Longevity: Instead of eating less, perhaps humans can live longer through mechanisms related to the insulin-like signaling system, a complex hormonal pathway that plays a vital role in regulating an organism's energy allocations. It is known that inactivating parts of the insulin-like signaling system through mutations extends life and delays senescence in flies, mice and worms. The operative molecule controlled by this system is the insulin-like growth factor-1 (IGF-1), a signaling protein whose name derives from the fact that the gene and protein have a significant sequence homology with insulin. However, this protein's functions are quite distinct from insulin's.

Apparently, the insulin-like signaling system can shift an organism's emphasis from growth to repair by modulating the IGF-1 level so as to activate or depress two diametrically opposed sets of genes. The growth set includes genes that bring about rapid body growth and a high reproductive rate. The stress-resistance set includes genes that make products that help an organism fight stress.

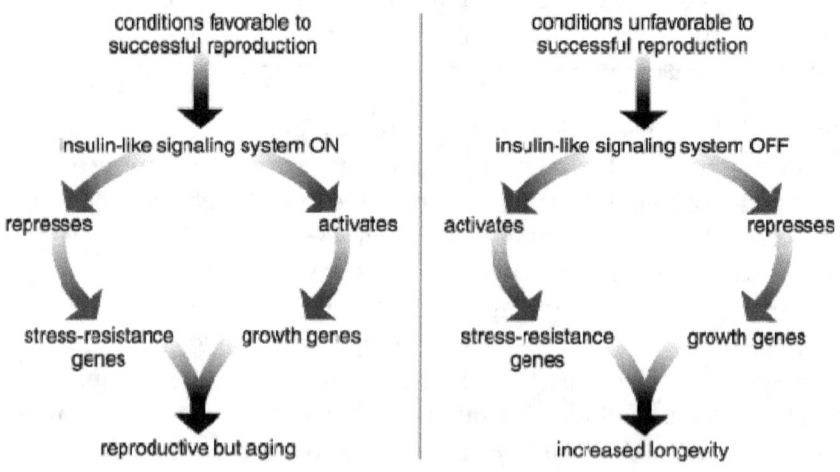

Figure 9.4. Environmental conditions influence aging. Conditions favorable to successful reproduction, such as a rich food supply and a dearth of potential competitors (in the case of nematodes) sparks the insulin-like signaling system. That system represses stress-resistance genes, which make products that help an organism fight stress, and activates growth genes, which stimulate rapid body growth and a high reproductive rate. As a result, an organism can reproduce well but ages quicker because it is not putting energy into maintenance. Conditions unfavorable to successful reproduction, on the other hand, repress the insulin-like signaling system, which turns off growth genes but turns on stress-resistance genes. That pattern supports increased longevity. So, switching metabolism from a pro-growth stance to a pro-repair stance by repressing the insulin-like signaling system might delay the onset of senescence in many organisms.

Under ordinary circumstances, it is a young organism's environment, including its diet that controls the insulin-like signaling system. Conditions favorable for reproduction indirectly cause the release of high levels of IGF-1, which activates the insulin-like signaling system. Then, the insulin-like signaling system represses the stress-resistance genes and activates the growth genes. Unfavorable conditions, on the other hand, indirectly lead to a low level of IGF-1 and repress the insulin-like signaling system, which activates the stress-resistance genes and represses the growth genes. So, switching metabolism from a pro-growth stance to a pro-repair stance by somehow repressing the insulin-like signaling system does delay the onset of senescence in many organisms, including mammals. This, of course, is exactly what Martin Holzenberger and his colleagues did in the experiment described above when they decreased the number of IGF-1 receptors by 50 percent and thus lowered the effective concentration of the signaling molecules.

Breath of Life and Death: Without oxygen, we cannot generate enough energy to live, and we quickly die. Nonetheless, oxygen also breaks down in cells to yield ROS molecules (Reactive oxygen species or ROS are chemically-reactive molecules containing oxygen). These reactive molecules combine with cellular components and transform them into oxygen-based damage products. This structural transformation alters a molecule's function, usually for the worse, and the damage process also generates another

ROS molecule. The destruction rampages through a cell until an antioxidant molecule stops the damage. In so-called oxidative stress, a cell essentially goes through self-perpetuating rusting.

Once breathed in, oxygen goes to mitochondria to help convert the energy from food to a chemical form that is useful to cells. Depending on energy needs, a cell might have from ten to several hundred mitochondria. With most of a cell's oxygen located in mitochondria, that is where most of a cell's ROS get generated. A mitochondrion's lipid membrane and protein enzymes serve as the nearest target for the ROS, but these components can be repaired. Mitochondria, though, are the only animal-cell organelles with their own genetic system, and the one to ten mitochondrial DNA molecules are very vulnerable to irreparable oxidative damage. Injured mitochondria soon become almost nonfunctional. The resulting energy shortage inhibits a cell's normal functioning, and tissues start aging.

Organisms can fight off oxidative stress, and young animals eliminate most, but not all, of the ROS molecules. Sooner or later, inefficiencies appear in an organism's defense mechanisms. Then, the rate of cell damage compounds, and the age-related loss of function soon becomes apparent. In studies of flies, mice and worms, aging proceeded faster than ever, after inactivating oxidative stress–resistance genes. Apparently, stress-resistance pathways function in a parallel but integrated manner with the insulin-like signaling system. This mitochondrial–free radical theory of aging explains much of what happens in aging laboratory model systems and in humans.

Many investigators realized that increasing the level of defense mechanisms against oxidative stress could extend an organism's health span. For example, several labs used genetic engineering to introduce extra copies of ROS-scavenging genes into otherwise normal flies, and the flies entered senescence later and lived longer, much like the artificially selected long-lived flies described above. Likewise, David Chavous of Boston College and his colleagues achieved similar results through the over expression of repair genes in flies, whose products repaired some proteins damaged by ROS. Working on worms, Pamela Larsen of the University of Southern California showed that up-regulating oxidative stress–resistance genes delayed the onset of senescence and created longer-lived animals; while Shuji Honda and Mitsuyoshi Matsuo of the Tokyo Metropolitan Institute of Gerontology demonstrated that higher-than-normal levels of oxygen accelerated the aging of both wild type and mutant animals.

Robert Arking's work on artificial selection in flies also produced organisms with a much higher level of oxidative-stress resistance and more efficient mitochondria. In fact, the lower level of oxidative damage and delayed onset of senescence in those flies arose from decreased production and increased destruction of ROS. However, using genetic-engineering techniques to insert extra copies of these same oxidative stress–resistance genes into mice has not yet resulted in extending longevity.

Science and Society: Although the genetic manipulations explored in the lab do not make likely therapeutic tools so far, the results encouraged many scientists to explore pharmaceutical attacks on aging. A variety of such experiments recorded significant increases in an animal's health span or a significant extension of an animal's functional abilities. For example, Semour Benzer and his team at the California Institute of Technology fed fruit flies a drug called 4-phenylbutyrate, which inhibits enzymes used by the cell to repress its stress-resistance genes, and it delayed the onset of senescence. Nonetheless, different strains of flies needed different drug doses in order to yield the same result. This implies the existence of genetically based individual differences in response to drug-based interventions to increase longevity.

Other types of pharmaceutical interventions are also being pursued. For instance, Simon Melov of the Buck Institute for Age Research and his colleagues gave worms drugs which that functioned as synthetic superoxide dismutase/catalase enzymes, or mimetics, and scavenge excess ROS within cells. The worms lived 44 percent longer, on average. So pharmaceutical interventions against aging seem feasible.

Nonetheless, people should mistrust the nonscientific claims and blarney put out by the present anti-aging industry. For example, at least 250,000 Web sites sell human growth hormone, and many tout it as a cure for aging. It is not. In the original study behind anti-aging claims for growth hormone, a dozen men showed positive effects at first, but then suffered deleterious side effects that cancelled the study. Now, scientific data suggest that taking growth hormone advances aging—quite the opposite from what the ads purport.

The future of aging research faces three significant questions. First, can science increase the health span of a laboratory primate? Second, will similar interventions extend human life in a safe way? Third, will public debate on this matter encourage or inhibit using this knowledge? Given the success of pharmaceuticals extending the health span of invertebrates, a similar outcome seems biologically reasonable in mammals, but proving that will take some time— definitely years, although no one knows how many. In monkeys, perhaps another decade will provide good data on whether interventions can slow the rate of aging, but it could take longer for a complete assessment of lifetime effects. The pace of discovery in this field, however, increases rapidly, so these time lines might be too conservative.

If someone finds a pharmaceutical that mimics the effects of caloric restriction or of IGF-1 reduction or of releasing the repression of stress-resistance genes, it might be possible to add about 25 years to a person's lifespan. Humans might then be healthy adults from the age of 20 to 80 years, instead of the current 20 to 55 or so. That sounds great to most people, but some critics see only increased despair and financial costs. This criticism, however, overlooks the fact that the senescent phase will stay the same in absolute terms, and the associated costs will not change. In fact, an increased health span will not cost more. Instead, it would give us longer, healthier and more productive lives.

Engineering the Age-related Genes

Genetic engineering has opened the possibility of transferring specific genes including the ones involved in aging, via bacterial *plasmid* or virus DNA. But in order to transfer a specific gene, we must learn the location and function of each gene (30,000 estimated in a human cell) along the double helix inside the center of every cell. Genetic mapping to study gene locations has progressed in the last decade and it is only a question of time until every chromosome will be known to contain the genes for specific enzymes. The map once completed, can provide geneticists with a catalogue of genes which can be used in genetic engineering. So, if aging is a function of certain specific genes and/or the result of genetic breakdown, it may ultimately be possible to transplant new genes that would enable older people to regain the level of vitality they had during youth.

How far we are from actually applying genetic engineering to stop aging is a difficult prediction to make. But scientists have started to implant mice with an enzyme-producing gene to see if it would make them live longer. Although the technology is developing very rapidly, research dealing with living organisms is not always straightforward. The important thing is that you do not have to wait for this genetic revolution or any other medical breakthrough. The important points emphasized in this guide to slow down aging and to feel healthy are based primarily on natural diet and health care (some based on our knowledge of aging process). Therefore, simple, safe, and practical hints exist for you to test for yourself.

Appendix 1

THE MAXIMUM VERIFIABLE LIFE SPANS FOR A NUMBER OF ANIMALS

Animal	Age (years)
Tortoise	150
Man	113
Asian Elephant	60
Gorilla	55
Chimpanzee	50
Golden eagle	50
Whale	50
Horse	40
Grizzly bear	35
Domestic cat	30
American buffalo	26
Lion	25
Rhesus monkey	24
Dolphin	23

Dog	20
Domestic goat	20
Moose	17
Kangaroo	16
Rabbit	15
Skunk	8
Rat	4
Mouse	3.50

About the Author

Dr. Sukhraj S. Dhillon has an advanced degree in life sciences and molecular biology from the west and a fascination with yoga, breathing, religion and spirituality from the east crafted out of studies at Yale University, U.S.A. and Punjab University, India. Therefore, he is uniquely qualified to present a synthesis of eastern and western approaches towards Health, Weight, Vegetarianism, Meditation, Yoga, Power of Now, Soul, God, science, and religion. He has published over 12 books and 40 research papers which include his work on **DNA and aging**; and has expressed his views in the news media and workshops. He has been the President, Chairman of the board, and life-trustee of a non-profit religious organization and has expressed his views in the congregation and at international seminars. Most of his titles are now available at **Amazon Kindle**, **Barnes & Noble** and other book sellers.